# Badger

Animal
Series editor: Jonathan Burt

# Badger

Daniel Heath Justice

REAKTION BOOKS

*To my father, Jimmie J Justice, for teaching me reverence*
*for the wild world and humility before its many mysteries.*
*Wado, Dad, now and always.*

Published by

REAKTION BOOKS LTD

33 Great Sutton Street

London EC1V 0DX, UK

www.reaktionbooks.co.uk

First published 2015

Printed and bound in China by 1010 Printing International Ltd

A catalogue record for this book is available from the British Library

ISBN 978 1 78023 336 9

# Contents

Kumagai Naohiko,
*Badger and Moon*,
Meiji era, late 19th
century, ink and
colour on silk.

# Beneath the Moon, Below the Earth: Considering Badgers

For if you finde a Badgerde abroad, it shall not be from hir burrow lightly.
George Gascoigne, *The noble arte of venerie or hunting* (1575)

I/am the offspring of the moon, her/pathway of light
the strip of white/on my forehead . . .
John W. Sexton, 'Badger' (2000)

Badgers hold a special place in the human imagination, but most of us have never seen one in person. Like most North Americans born and raised in the pre-Internet age, my early interactions with badgers were largely literary, with Kenneth Grahame's very British Mr Badger being the most prominent acquaintance. (Today's youth are more likely to know the Internet meme of Randall's 'Crazy Nastyass Honey Badger' better than Grahame's rather fusty forest recluse, even in the UK.) Though I now live in Canada, I was the third generation of my mother's family raised in the working-class mining town of Victor, Colorado, and literature was my escape from the region's many hardships. Given the ubiquitous reminders of the area's gold rush history, from innumerable tunnels and tailings piles scattered across the rocky landscape to the weathered ruins of the mines themselves, even at a young age I was an avid reader of fantastical tales about delving dwarves, burrow-dwelling hobbits and other subterranean peoples. It was therefore natural and perhaps even inevitable that badgers and their symbolic kin would intrigue me. (It wasn't until I was older that I would discover that the iconic literary badgers with which I was most familiar were of the Eurasian variety, *Meles meles*, rather than the distinctive North American species, *Taxidea taxus*.) There was something disquieting but enormously appealing in the idea of the hollowed-out earth under my feet being a secret realm inhabited by various natural and supernatural entities.

Yet I never actually encountered a living badger when I was growing up. My experience with them was limited to their diggings in local mountain meadows where our friends' cattle grazed, or the occasional full-body preserved mount on display in a nearby antique store, gun shop or museum. Where familiarity was absent, imagination ran wild, and badgers became something more than my real animal neighbours – they became evocative symbols of ancient tradition, representatives of rooted stability and guardians of the earth's deep mysteries. (Had J. K. Rowling's *Harry Potter* series been published at that time, I would have certainly been a Hufflepuff House partisan and proud supporter of its Eurasian badger mascot.)

Even if I had been brought up with the traditional stories of my father's people, badgers are not among the common animals of Cherokee tradition, and I certainly never heard about badgers in association with the Ute peoples on whose homeland we lived. It was not until many years later that I met living badgers and began to learn something of their own complex personalities and habits. Yet in the very first of those meetings I learned at least as much about human attitudes toward these shy creatures as about badgers themselves.

MEETING FRANCES

I went to visit Frances in Oklahoma City on a sweltering June morning during one of my annual summer trips to Cherokee and Chickasaw country. I had driven in from Tulsa the previous night during a terrifying thunderstorm. Morning dawned with little evidence of the tempest, but I was worried that the heavy

*Fig. 61*

*Fig. 62*

*Fig. 63*

Fig 61 Die gemeine Dachs (*Meles Taxus*)
Fig 62 Die Telodu oder javanische Stinkdachs (*Mydaus melceps*)
Fig 63 Die Chinga oder das Hudsonische Stinkthier (*Mephitis Chinga*)

Eurasian badger, stink badger and skunk from Georges Cuvier's *Le Règne animal* (1828).

rain and resulting mud would scuttle my long-awaited meeting with Frances, the resident North American badger of the Oklahoma City Zoo.

Laura Bottaro, the zoo's Curator of Mammals, had already warned me that Frances might not be amenable to a visit. Much of the outdoor enclosure was visible, but the largely nocturnal Frances was skittish around humans and could be hiding in the dark recesses beneath the elevated walkway. Early morning was the best time to visit, so I drove into the zoo's parking lot just before 9 a.m., hoping to beat the crowds and catch Frances on a good day, as I had only a few hours available before my flight back to Canada.

Laura met me at the gate and we first drove in a golf cart then walked to the beginning of the Oklahoma Trails exhibit, which features more than a hundred animals native to Oklahoma in enclosures based on the state's various ecological zones. After passing a mountain lion, Mexican grey wolves, swift foxes and white-tailed deer, we came to the tall-grass prairie zone, where Frances lived alongside prairie dogs in an adjoining area and at least three bison in the expansive space on the other side. At first it seemed that the storm had ruined my plans, for the ground was now churned to a sloppy soup of red earth. But as we stepped onto the walkway, Laura pointed to a stone bench in the enclosure below, where Frances lay, mud-spattered forepaws folded beneath her, sleepily surveying her little domain.

I remained there for more than an hour, sometimes taking pictures but more often just watching with barely contained glee, until the stream of passers-by and the increasing heat and humidity of the morning proved to be too distracting to us both. Frances lay under the bench for about 20 minutes before she began trotting around the enclosure. Sometimes she gave a predatory sniff at the Plexiglass that separated her from the

neighbouring prairie dogs. Once she squatted in a little latrine area at the far end, and occasionally entered the tunnels beneath the walkway. But she always returned to view. Laura's colleague Jeff Rife arrived to feed Frances two freshly killed mice as I watched with camera ready. When she had finished and it was clear that no more food was forthcoming, Frances crouched with

Frances, resident badger of the Oklahoma City Zoo, 2010.

her fur standing on end, bared her canines and gave a defiant hiss, then returned to her spot beneath the bench to calmly groom the mud from her claws.

Not long before I left the zoo, I watched as a family leisurely strolled up the walkway to look at the various prairie animals. They stopped briefly at the transparent barrier that revealed Frances's enclosure. By that time she had returned to lie in the shadowed nook under her bench. A young boy of about three released his father's hand to see what mysterious creature lived below. To my surprise, he recoiled in disgust and rushed back to his father. 'Badger mean!' he pouted, grabbing his father's leg. The man nodded distractedly and responded, 'Yeah, really mean', before meandering with his family towards the bison. The boy's excited squeal seemed to indicate that those massive ungulates were more to his liking.

It was a brief encounter, but one that still exemplifies some of the competing attitudes that define human–badger interactions. For me, Frances was a fascinating, even evocative being who moved with surprising and unanticipated grace, and who quite clearly had an independent mind of her own. For the boy and his father, however, she was just 'mean', a vicious beast deserving of far less regard than the more dramatic animals elsewhere in the zoo. We were all looking at the same creature, but what we actually saw could not have been more different.

Whether beneath the moon or below the earth, whether living, legendary or entirely imaginary, badgers inhabit the shadowy underworld of our fantasies and the material world of open grasslands, temperate woodlands and tropical jungles, desert expanses, back gardens and even rubbish-strewn alleys. They have inherited a rich legacy of symbolism from their human neighbours, but they also carry the dangerous burden of our misconceptions and

Eurasian badger drinking from a pool.

disregard. The various badger species and their relatives can be found on all continents except Antarctica, South America and Oceania, have shared territory and resources with *Homo sapiens* since our evolutionary rise, and continue to figure in the traditional stories, religious practices and arts of many human cultures, yet the closest most of us will ever come to badgers is through their proxies in popular culture.

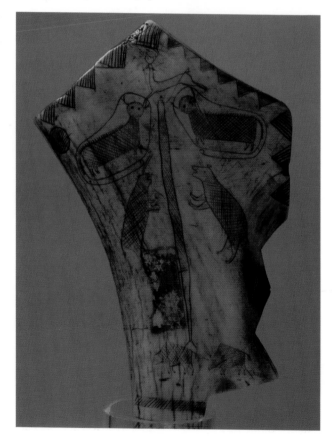

Winnebago (Ho-Chunk) ceremonial club with etched badgers.

This is not particularly surprising: badgers are generally nocturnal and almost invariably wary of humans. Like many predator species, they thrive best where human settlement and persecution are limited. And while pelts, skulls, teeth, claws, full-body mounts and other taxidermic remains are to be found in museum display cases and on shelves in homes throughout the world, there are relatively few places to see living badgers in person: the African honey badger (*Mellivora capensis*) and Asian hog badger (*Arctonyx collaris*) could match any of their geographic counterparts for striking physical features, but they are unsuited to life in captivity, and for zoo audiences they do not share the iconic capital of the more celebrated and more often encountered elephants, pandas and tigers.

This book is concerned with two enmeshed subjects of enquiry: the flesh-and-blood badgers of natural history, and the

Honey badger, or ratel.

much more evasive creatures of human symbol, story and art. Badgers inhabit a richly varied world all their own, one that has shaped their evolution since their primaeval weasel ancestors moved from the forest's sun-pierced canopy to its shadowed roots. And yet for thousands of years they have been confronted by the decidedly mixed legacy of being so fascinating and occasionally even fearsome to some of their hominid neighbours. Formidable avatars of nature's defiant spirit or pestilential threats to cattle, crops and other wildlife, badgers have been admired and reviled with equal passion throughout our shared history.

Stop-motion figure of Mr Badger, voiced by Sir Michael Hordern, from Cosgrove Hall's *Wind in the Willows* television films and series, 1983–9.

*Badger* traces the complex and contradictory ways in which this animal endures in both the human imagination and the other-than-human world. Here we consider a sampling of the badger's life and lore, from its evolution and widespread distribution to its current and often imperilled status throughout the world, from its natural history and life in the wild to the folklore, legends and spiritual beliefs it inspires, to its representation in the arts and exploitation in various industries. Given these many different layers of significance and how little most of us actually know about them, real badgers are too often interpreted through or erased by our own culturally projected anxieties and presumptions. There is still much to learn about these misunderstood creatures, but to do so, we must begin as close as possible to the animals themselves, untangling some of what we think we know from what might be nearer the truth of their own lived experiences.

Klaus Pichler, *Monkey, Badger, Mirror*, 2010.

# 1 Natural Histories of the Badger

The reasons must bee strong, that shall perswade
Me under ground: The Badger loves his hole,
Yet is not so bashfull, but dares looke out
And shew himselfe, when there is prey abroad . . .
William Davenant, *Britannia triumphans* (1637)

A MISUNDERSTOOD MUSTELID

Humans might well be called *Homo discribens*, the classifying human. We define things, sort them into categories based on perceived relationships, qualities, functions and ideals. Some taxonomies – classification systems – are more functional, problematic or arbitrary than others, but all reflect our desire to make sense of the world and our place in it. Yet the staggering diversity of the natural world defies our attempts at a fully knowable order, and the solid definitions of one generation often crumble with the next. And sometimes the definitions are always in flux.

A case in point: what is a badger? The answer is more complicated and contested than we might initially think. Badgers confound our categories. They are unlike other creatures, strangely complete in themselves though seemingly an admixture of qualities and features belonging to more familiar beasts. So in asking what defines a badger, we can be assured that the answer will challenge our expectations as well. First, it depends on geography, for the badgers of the United Kingdom are not the same creatures referred to by that name in Kenya, Indonesia or Canada. Some scientists see only three genera as legitimate bearers of the name, while many identify four or more. (And this does not include the divergent opinions on the number of badger subspecies around the world, from around a dozen to nearly 40.) Similarly, the English

Eurasian badger in forest.

Francis Barlow, *Badger, c.* 17th century.

word offers little help and much to ponder: though the precise etymology is unclear, *badger* is most likely just a simple reference to the 'badge', the facial pelage (coat) patterning of the Eurasian and North American members of the clan, which is reminiscent of the bold device worn by medieval knights for identification at a distance.[1] The oft-cited claim that the English term comes from the French *bêcheur*, 'digger' (specifically, a human at labour with a shovel or spade), seems to be a case of folk etymology based on the word's superficial association with badger behaviour. *Bêcheur* is certainly old, dating to at least 1453 and thus pre-dating recorded uses of the English *badger* (around 1525). But the martial term *badge* is older still, with a confirmed history to 1440. Further, there is less evidence for *bêcheur* as a historical reference than for the more consistently specific and prominent French name for the animal, *blaireau*, which goes back to 1312, pre-dating all these terms. *Bêcheur* is thus a possible candidate for today's *badger* but less plausible than the simpler root of 'badge'.[2]

Other definitions are alternately vague, vexed or simply insufficient. Names aside, humans have long debated the nature

A Eurasian badger furtively observes a passing knight in Emil Reinicke's satirical *Der Schnappshahn*, c. 19th century, oil on canvas.

CONTRARIETATES CAVENDAS ·

Sextus Placitus, *De medina ex animalibus*, 12th-century manuscript.

of the creature itself, particularly its relationship to other animals, given its unique physiology and habits. For many years, as we shall see, badgers were understood to be a small relative of bears or a type of dog or pig, and in some traditions they still maintain a spiritual kinship with bears; species once considered in the badger family are now disputed or entirely exiled from the clan, while others are still within the larger definition in spite of biological distinctiveness. In all cases, there is much that remains unclear and contested about this beast we call a badger.

If we look to scientific classifications, the simplest definition we have today is that a badger is a fossorial (digging) carnivore of the larger weasel family, the mustelids (Mustelidae). The inclusion of the Eurasian badger (*Meles*), North American badger (*Taxidea*) and hog badger (*Arctonyx*) in the category of 'true' badger is generally settled, with some debate among zoologists about the distantly related ferret badgers (*Melogale*) and even less consensus on the status of the more genetically divergent but better known honey badger or ratel (*Mellivora*). Stink badgers (*Mydaus* and *Suillotaxus*), once considered part of the extended badger clan, are now located in the skunk family. The question of definition is complex, and what we understand the term to mean continues to change according to expanding research. So we start this journey at one of many possible beginnings. Whatever the truth of badgers' evolutionary and natural history, humans have offered varied speculations on their roots and relations.

DOGS, HOGS AND BEARS

There are surprisingly few traditional stories about the origins of badgers – they seem to have always been around, solid and certain in their belonging to the lands they call home. It is in the genre of natural history that the question of origins (and therefore

Caapse Ratel. Sheer op hye netten gesteld, Destrikeart het boel rest stadye lyen, an honing-
18° leer byn hort vel moejelyk dan de honden te donden.

Rijnlandse Maat.

Robert Jacob Gordon, *Caapse Ratel* (*Cape Ratel*), c. 1772–80, pen, ink and pencil.

connections) becomes significant. Because the Eurasian badger is the template for the species in global iconography, we begin our search for badger origins by looking to the natural histories of the ancient Mediterranean, but there we will find little clarity. The Greek historian Herodotus may have made reference to a honey badger in his fifth-century BCE account of 'a ferocious animal in the deserts of India, larger than a fox and smaller than a dog, which digs for gold in the sands', but the argument, while compelling, remains speculative.[3] (According to Aristotle, Herodotus also said that badgers were hermaphroditic and impregnated themselves, which the philosopher dismissed as 'another silly and extremely wrong-headed story'.[4]) Similarly, the Roman naturalist Pliny the Elder is of no real help in his *Natural History*, a text that blends careful direct observation with the rather more dubious contributions of travellers' tales and fanciful speculation. Aside from claiming that the monstrous (and mythical) leucrocotta includes the head of a she-badger among its hybrid features, Pliny reports that fearful Eurasian badgers inhale so deeply that their skin swells to repel attacks from dogs and hunters – a classical description of what would later be known as the blood sport of badger-baiting, wherein a badger is forced to fight to its death against an onslaught of dogs.[5]

A subsequent chronicler, the medieval monk Giraldus Cambrensis (Gerald of Wales), provides the following imaginative description of their burrowing habits in his *Topographia hibernica* (*The Topography and Natural History of Ireland*):

> There is also here the badger or melot, an unclean animal, which bites sharply, frequenting the mountains and rocks.

Fanciful image of badgers in cooperative sett excavation from the *Harley Bestiary*, c. 1230–40.

A badger among other beasts in Gerald of Wales's *Topographia hibernica*, c. 1220.

It makes holes under ground for its refuge and protection, scratching and digging them out with its feet. Some of them, whose natural instinct it is to serve the rest, have been seen, to the great admiration of the observers, lying on their backs with the earth dug out heaped on their bellies, and held together by their four claws, while others dragged them backward by a stick held in their mouth, fastening their teeth in which, they drew them out of the hole, with their burthens.[6]

Here, as in Pliny and the work of later medieval commentators, the focus is on supposed behaviour and symbolic significance, especially as they fit existing religious and philosophical presumptions about the natural world.

In the centuries that followed, the most common European explorations of animal subjects were religious, with animals serving as instructional representatives of particular human virtues or vices. To the medieval European world, animals were objects whose purposes were largely instrumental (as food, clothing and commodity), social (through companionship as pets and providing service and status through hunting or husbandry) and symbolic (through art, story and tradition). Badgers only rarely appear in the allegorical representations of medieval bestiaries. More often they are to be found in hunting texts of the time, and generally as a lesser quarry marked by the vices of sloth, lust and gluttony.

Clarity of animal origins became more important to natural philosophers in Europe during the early modern period. This was fuelled in part by rediscovered classical texts and newly encountered Islamic works on history, philosophy, science and medicine, as well as the booty of extractive colonial expeditions throughout Asia, Africa, the Pacific and the Americas. The world was gradually but irreversibly transformed by the intentional as well as inadvertent exchange of thousands of plants and animals between continents and complex, often violent encounters between thousands of human cultures through global colonialism from 1492 onwards. Yet it was the frenzy for definitions that accompanied imperialist expansion and scientific and social revolution during the seventeenth- and eighteenth-century Enlightenment that brought badgers and other beings into European focus as more than moral symbols or useful body parts. Developing a systematic and ostensibly universal taxonomy for the various plants, minerals, beasts and even other humans of the ever-larger and more diverse world in part fulfilled their God's mandate to Adam – symbolically, if not in fact – whereby humans were granted the power to name and thus define and, not incidentally, dominate all elements of creation. Definition

Badger and other mammals from Georges Cuvier's *Le Règne animal* (1828).

26

was thus an intellectual, ideological and economic imperative of the European Enlightenment.

The criteria for such definitions, however, have often changed. A sporting manual of the late seventeenth century makes the then-common argument that there are 'two sorts of *Badgers, Dog-Badgers*, as resembling a *Dog* in his Feet; and a *Hog-Badger*, as resembling a *Hog* in his cloven hoofs', further insisting that the two kinds 'differ in their Food, the one eating *Flesh* and *Carion* like a *Dog*, and the other *Roots* and Fruits like a *Hog*' as well as their habitations, with the former preferring inaccessible woodlands and mountains and the latter, 'being fat and lazy', earthing in 'open, easy and light grounds'.[7] For both, 'the young ones are called Pigs, the *Male* is called the *Boar*, and the *Female* the *Sow*'.[8] This fanciful account assigns species distinction where none exists, as the author is clearly referring to Eurasian badgers living in different habitats. Europeans would not encounter the animal we know today as the hog badger until the eighteenth century.

More significant than supposed kinship to canines and swine, however, is the association of badgers with bears, a connection that will often emerge in this book. Throughout the world and in many different and distinct cultural contexts, wherever badgers and bears have been found together, they have often been presumed to be related, as both groups share a number of physical features: a hunched and stocky profile, non-retractable claws, coarse fur, wedge-shaped head and well-muscled body, with a forceful defence when threatened and a reputedly high pain threshold that was frequently tested by the popular practice of both bear- and badger-baiting, especially in the UK. Their biological habits are also similar, such as winter torpor (though no members of any bear or badger species practise true hibernation), omnivorous diet and the ability by females to delay implantation of fertilized eggs. The pig association partly returns in contem-

Meles Labradoria Sabine .
*Ursus Taxus Schreb.*

porary terminology, at least in Europe, as for bears and Eurasian badgers alike the adult males are boars and females are sows (though their offspring are cubs, not piglets).

In 1758 the father of contemporary scientific classification, Carl Linnaeus, included both Eurasian badgers and American raccoons among the bears in family *Ursus*. (Linnaeus did not refer to the North American species of badger, but subsequent scientists continued the bear classification, such as the German naturalist Johann Christian Daniel von Schreber's designation of the species as *Ursus taxus* in 1777.) Nearly 60 years after Linnaeus's initial classification, the influential French naturalist Georges Cuvier published his four-volume *Le Règne animal distribué d'après son organisation* (*The Animal Kingdom, Arranged According to its*

*Organization*), and placed bears, badgers, raccoons, pandas, kinkajous, coatis, 'gluttons' (wolverines) and honey badgers (ratels) in the same 'tribe' – Plantigrada – defined largely by their shared habit of walking 'on the whole of the foot'.[9] In the first (1790) and second (1791) editions of Thomas Bewick's *A General History of Quadrupeds* there is no reference to the badger's Linnaean classification, but by the fourth edition in 1800 the Eurasian badger was explicitly labelled a type of bear – *Ursus meles* – though a 'very harmless and inoffensive' one.[10]

The question of badger origins continued to provoke debate three-quarters of a century later. 'Since the extirpation of the Bear, *Ursus arctos*, of the existence of which mention is made in Scottish history as late as the year 1073', writes Thomas Bell in *A History of British Quadrupeds*, 'the family of the *Ursidæ* has had no other representative, in our indigenous zoology, than the present animal [badger], which in its habits, no less than in its structure, claims no very remote relationship with that tribe'. By the 1870s there was increasing evidence that badgers were, in fact, members of the extended mustelid (weasel) family, but so established was the belief in the badger-as-bear hypothesis among late nineteenth-century naturalists that the second edition of Bell's book still placed badgers among the *Ursidae*, with the following odd caveat:

> Since the above was written, the genus *Meles* has been shown to possess intimate zoological affinities with the *Mustelidæ*. Our friend Mr Waterhouse – perhaps the highest existing authority on what relates to Mammalia – has traced gradations through a series of genera, from *Meles* to *Mustela*; but as we believe in certain points of relationship between the *Mustelidæ* and the *Ursidæ*, we, for the present, shall retain the Badger in the latter family.[11]

'For the present' did not last long. By the end of the nineteenth century the mustelid affiliation of the Eurasian badger was largely accepted, and the bearish *Ursus meles* was no more: the weasel relative *Meles meles* had taken its place.

## MUSTELIDAE: THE WEASELS

For zoologists today, the biological family to which the various badger genera belong is Mustelidae, the mustelids: weasels and their various kin, including otters, wolverines, mink, ferrets, martens, fishers and polecats. Part of the largest group of predators in the mammalian order Carnivora, these diverse animals have evolved to live in nearly every geographic terrain, from tundra and boreal forest to river, ocean, temperate woodland, tropical

Hand-coloured engraving of Eurasian badgers in W. MacGillivray's *British Quadrupeds* (1828).

PLATE 9.

*Stewart del.*     *Lizars sc.*

THE BADGER.

jungle and savannah, to take maximum advantage of many habitats, climates and prey species.

Yet these categories are under constant revision, rendering the taxonomic accuracy of any study such as this one temporary at best, as mustelids continue to evade easy classification. While skunks used to be considered part of the musk-producing weasel family, in a case not unlike that of the 'badger as bear' debate most researchers now place skunks within their own family, Mephitidae. Stink badgers (*Mydaus*) are now generally affiliated with the skunk family due to genetic similarities, a shared common ancestor and pronounced anatomical differences from other mustelids. Similarly, the tree-climbing ferret badgers (*Melogale*), previously thought closest to the original marten-like form from which true badgers evolved, are increasingly distanced from true badgers and associated with the sleeker weasel-like carnivores of the subfamily *Helictidinae*.[12] Yet Charles A. Long and Carl Arthur Killingley caution against assuming too fixed an interpretation of badger origins and development, as 'the evolution of badgers cannot yet be fully explained because the fossil record is sketchy and the use of characters in our samples can lead to several interpretations.'[13]

There is clearly much yet to be learned and many mysteries about badger origins remain. Nevertheless, a picture has emerged that seems generally consistent as more evidence is unearthed in the fossil record and as advances in genetic science reveal histories and connections only hypothesized before.

PREHISTORIC BADGERS

About 23 million years ago, during the Neogene period, major shifts in climate and geography diminished the dense forest canopy in favour of more open terrain. The widespread change in habitat spurred different members of the weasel family to branch off in divergent evolutionary lines: some remained in the trees, some took to the waters, and others headed to the earth to become various land predators, including the ancestors of today's badgers.[14] Given the great lengths of time, there are substantial gaps in the fossil record and variability in the current data, but the following seems a reasonable assessment of the evolutionary history.[15] About 20 million years ago, in the Miocene epoch, the first badgers to appear were the direct ancestors of *Taxidea*, the North American badger, which emerged in Asia before establishing itself in what is now northern Mexico, the u.s. and Canada. *Taxidea* has a solid place in the fossil record, as does its extinct

Nobu Tamura's rendering of *Chamitataxus avitus*, a prehistoric ancestor of the North American badger.

33

relatives, *Pliotaxidea* and *Chamitataxus*, which lived about six million years ago.[16] Another split in the evolutionary line began from around 3 to 10 million years ago, and it was during this time that the ancestors of the three other badger groups (*Meles*, the Eurasian badger, *Arctonyx*, the hog badger, and *Mellivora*, the honey badger) emerged and began their gradual inhabitation of an ever-changing land base.[17] The early Eurasian badger gradually surrendered the increasingly warm, tropical regions of its extended range to the hog badger, which flourished in that habitat. The fossil history of the more genetically distant honey badger is still very much a mystery, but all available evidence indicates that its presence in Africa has been a long one, dating millions of years earlier than those of Eurasian or hog badgers.[18]

In short, as the land and plants transformed, so too did the mustelids, and the various badger-kin began the slow crawl of millions of years down from the treetops in pursuit of earthbound prey. Much changed for badgers as they moved from the forms we can construct or conjecture by their fossilized remains to the living, breathing creatures of today: size, shape, distribution, territory. But one thing has remained consistent across all these changes, times and geographies and contributed to their endurance: they have always been effective and efficient predators.

TEETH, CLAWS . . . AND GLANDS?

Mustelids do not have the romantic reputations of carnivores like the big cats, wolves and bears. Aside from the 'cuter' mustelids like ferrets and otters, today most weasel-kin are far more likely than these more imposing predators to be dismissed as simple vermin or treated as vicious curiosities.[19] Predator species tend to evoke strong and often negative human emotions, for reasons ranging from competition for prey and fear of livestock or property destruction to the projection of our own cultural values and fears onto animal behaviour. Indeed, it may be an existential reaction. In those cultures that sharply distinguish humanity from the natural world, thus asserting an essential human superiority, antagonism towards predator species may well be a deeply fearful rejection of our own fundamentally animal nature.[20]

Certainly, mustelids are well equipped for hunting and killing prey, with keen senses, powerful jaws and claws specialized for breaking bones and rending flesh, and skeletal structures and musculature perfectly suited to the specific qualities of prey and vagaries of habitat. In practice, however, many mustelid diets are quite varied. For example, badgers are often omnivorous; in some regions, earthworms and other invertebrates make up a substantial portion of the diet of the Eurasian and hog badgers, and although the North American and honey badgers are the most consistently carnivorous of all badgers and badger-kin, they too vary their diet depending on available resources.

Yet it is not only their predatory proclivities that some humans find distasteful about mustelids. They also challenge our olfactory aesthetics – in a word, they stink. All mustelids have anal glands that emit an oily substance with a powerful smell; this was one of the characteristics that led the skunk to be classified as a mustelid for so long. In addition, there is a subcaudal (under the tail) gland unique to badgers, 'the largest scent gland described in any carnivore'.[21] In 2011 I had an opportunity to photograph two North American badgers at a wildlife sanctuary in Ontario, Canada. The handlers moved the badgers from their familiar enclosure to a different area to facilitate the photo shoot, and although unharmed the animals responded to the stressful experience by covering their hindquarters with their own secretions and bluff-charging us. The heavy, pungent smell of their subcaudal expulsions was not unlike that of burning rubber and it lingered long after I had

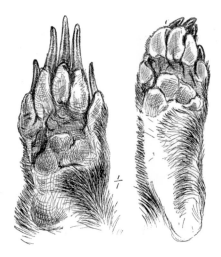

Ernest Thompson Seton's drawing of a North American badger's distinctive paws. From *Life-histories of Northern Animals*, 1909.

left the sanctuary. (This musking ability has been documented in other badger species: one commentator observed a fleeing ratel using these 'chemical defences' to disorientate four pursuing hyenas, allowing it the opportunity to escape.[22])

Besides self-protection, there are other vital uses for this odoriferous musk, along with other secretions such as urine, faeces and even earwax, as scent is one of the primary ways badgers navigate their habitat and social existence.[23] For the Eurasian badger, the fluid released from the subcaudal glands functions for targeted communication within and beyond the social group. The connections between badgers and their excretions extend even into human language: there may be a linguistic relationship between the ancient Hittite word *tašku-* (from which the Latin root for badger, *taxo*, is possibly descended) and its musky meanings of 'anus' or 'scrotum'.[24]

Numerous qualities and features identify badgers as mustelids, but the most significant characteristic that sets badgers apart from other weasel-kin is their trademark digging proclivities. All

Woodcut of a badger from Moriz Jung's *Animal ABC*, c. 1906.

badgers are proficient earth-delvers: this, more than anything, distinguishes them among mustelids, though the results of their efforts reflect varying degrees of complexity and permanence. From the temporary burrows and rodent extractions of the North American badger and African honey badger, the jungle-floor rootings of the hog badgers of tropical Asia, or the often elaborate, multigenerational setts of the Eurasian badger, the behaviour of badgers is shaped, to varying degrees, by their evolution for living and hunting in different subterranean habitats.

So, too, is their anatomy. Badgers are generally wide-bodied and well muscled, with stout necks and strong jaws; they trundle forward on broad feet equipped with long and sturdy claws, less graceful to human eyes than ferrets or otters but perfectly suited to their needs (and certainly deceptive to those who might underestimate their speed or agility). Their tough skins are difficult to penetrate and are covered in coarse hair that sheds dirt easily and, due to its dramatic patterning, may serve either warning or recognition purposes.[25]

Although there continues to be debate about which creatures should actually be considered true badgers due to divergences in biology, genetics and anatomy scientists generally agree on three species: the Eurasian badger, the Asian hog badger and the North American badger. More controversial is the honey badger, which is both genetically and genealogically distant from the others, though this species is generally still included among badger-kin.[26] I have chosen to limit the scope of my consideration to those genera most commonly associated with the term: namely, *Meles*, the common Eurasian badger; *Taxidea*, the North American badger; and *Mellivora*, the African ratel or honey badger, the distinctive relative of other badgers that fills their ecological niche throughout Africa and parts of India and Asia. While many researchers still include ferret badgers in the family, they remain marginal in the literature and are behaviourally quite different from their more prominent kin, and are largely excluded from this study. Given the comparative scarcity of available research and lore, I offer only a few observations on *Arctonyx*, the rare and furtive hog badger, although its firm place in the badger family is uncontested.[27]

The category of 'badger', then, loosely encompasses a small number of distinct but distantly related species that share certain anatomical and behavioural characteristics. It therefore offers a guiding conceptual principle, not a precise definitional boundary.[28] Indeed, the word 'badger' has long been used in this way by English-speaking travellers to refer to mammals in other lands that resembled the Eurasian badger in form or habit, such as the rock hyrax, the rock wallaby and the wombat.[29] In the seventeenth century, for example, even the six-banded armadillo of South America was inexplicably considered by Europeans to be a type of deer-killing badger.[30]

We have surveyed the controversies and broad contours of badger definition in the sciences, but before moving into the

realm of human kinship and imagination, we should give a bit more specialized attention to the main branches of the badger family thus defined.

Profile view of a Eurasian badger (*Meles meles*).

In Old English and Gaelic the ancient word for the Eurasian badger (*Meles meles*) was *broc* (a reference to its grey coloration), and today among some Britons the creatures remain the sett-dwelling *brock*. Among the Germans they are *Dachs* (and the dogs bred to hunt and harass them, *Dachshund*, *Dackel* or *Teckel*), while to the Dutch, they are *das*. As noted earlier, *blaireau* is the term in modern French. Drawing on the Latin root *taxo*, in Italian badgers are *tasso*, and in Portuguese, *teixugo*; the Catalan is *toixó*, while in Castilian it is *tejón* (which in Mexico refers specifically to the North American species, or even to the coati, a relative of the raccoon). In Norway it is *grevling*, meaning 'digger', with

39

variations of the term in Sweden and Denmark.[31] The Indigenous Sami peoples of northern Europe call them *mádár*, while in the tongue of their Finnish neighbours the term is *mäyrä*. Among Albanians, they are *vjedhulle*, meaning either 'thief' or 'fatty'; to Russians, they are *Барсук*; in Mandarin Chinese the name is pronounced *huān*, a homophone for the word for 'happiness' (and badgers are thus generally associated with good luck). The pale Japanese species is known as *anaguma* or *mujina*.

Tsukioka Yoshitoshi, *Badger Protects Its Cubs from Attack by a Dog* (likely a representation of the Japanese racoon dog rather than badgers), c. 1875, woodblock print.

Of all badgers, the common Eurasian species is the most recognizable and most widely represented in popular culture, and its striking markings provide the English name for the entire extended family. Although most of its hunchbacked body is grizzled grey-black (sometimes brown, more rarely dusty grey-white and, very occasionally, albino or all black), it is characterized most by its 'badge': a bold white stripe stretching up the face from the broad nose to the shoulders, and down the front and sides of the muzzle, neck and chest. When combined with long claws, broad paws, muscular, wedge-shaped form and digging behaviour, the badge distinguishes the Eurasian badger from other regional carnivores.

Found from the United Kingdom to the Arctic Circle, across Asia and even to Japan, the Eurasian badger has the widest distribution of any of its kin. Numerous species (one to three) and subspecies (four to 23) are found across that range, but as with all issues relating to badger taxonomy, Eurasian badger divisions are under constant debate and revision.[32] Males and females are roughly the same size, although boars are broader in head, neck and body than sows. A fully grown Eurasian badger can reach almost 100 cm (roughly 40 in.) in length from the tip of the stubby tail to the end of its sensitive nose, and can weigh between 10 and 20 kg (22–44 lb); they are among the largest wild creatures in the UK. (A mature badger has very little to fear from even the largest fox.)

It was the behaviour rather than the biology of *Meles* that most interested early European naturalists, though these categories were often conflated. For example, some commentators of the time, such as Edward Topsell in his popular *Historie of Fourefooted Beastes* (1607), repeated the popular but erroneous belief that the legs on one side of a badger's body were shorter than those on the other, due in part to its walking along hillsides. (The

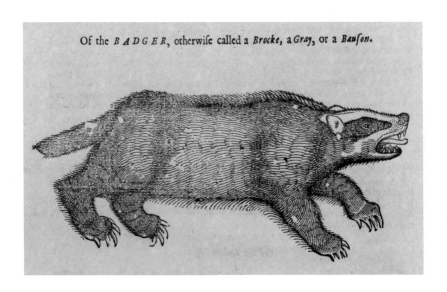

Of the *B A D G E R*, otherwife called a *Brocke*, a *Gray*, or a *Baufon*.

'Of the BADGER, otherwise called a *Brocke*, a *Gray*, or a *Bauson*', wood-cut from Edward Topsell's *The History of Four-footed Beasts and Serpents* (1658 edn).

badger in that volume's accompanying woodcut, however, displays no such misalignment.) In *A Description of the Nature of Four-Footed Beasts* (1678), the physician John Johnston did not mention asymmetrical limbs, but offered claims that were just as fanciful, including one of a novel way of escaping hunters: 'When they are spied, and hunted on hills, they lay their forelegs over their head, and [lie] round like a globe, and as Bears tumbled down.'[33] Nearly a century later, in his influential *Histoire naturelle* (*Natural History: General and Particular*), Georges-Louis Leclerc, the Comte de Buffon, moved away from the more imaginative descriptions but was unable to avoid moralizing claims that were equally discon-nected from objective observation:

> The Badger is an indolent, diffident, solitary animal. He retires to the most secret places, to the inmost recesses of the forest, and there digs a subterranean habitation. He

seems to fly society, and even the light, and spends three fourths of life in his dark abode, from which he never departs but in quest of subsistence. As his body is long, his legs short, his claws, especially those of the fore-feet, very long and strong, he digs and penetrates the earth with greater facility than any other animal.[34]

Contrary to Buffon's depiction of the badger as reclusive loner, the Eurasian badger is the most consistently social of all badgers. While in some circumstances *Meles* can be solitary and nomadic and spend only a season in a particular location, most Eurasian badgers live in family clans (called cetes) of a few to a dozen or more, inhabiting a well-defined socializing and subsistence territory that is anchored by the centrepiece of the community's life: the sett, a complex and often labyrinthine tunnel network that may include from a handful to dozens of entrances, tunnels and chambers. Some setts also provide shelter for other species, including carnivore competitors: red foxes have been observed to take up residence in unused chambers, with little conflict providing that they avoid the badgers' cubs.[35]

The sett is the heart of the Eurasian badger's world: it provides safety from weather and predators (humans armed with shovels and dogs are a notable exception), a secure place for breeding and reproduction, and a lightless but well-ventilated location for social interaction. Eurasian badgers harvest a wide range of both dry and fresh vegetation for bedding, depending on the season, which they carry back with great care and replace when soiled, rotten (if originally collected green) or parasite-ridden. Setts can be temporary, but in secure locations most are multigenerational and expand over time; indeed, some rare setts show evidence of successive badger habitation for hundreds and, amazingly, even thousands of years.[36]

Spending most of their lives in this underground network of tunnels, Eurasian badgers are most active above ground at night, where their comparatively poor eyesight is of no great disadvantage. Even in daylight badgers can be found snuffling through the forest undergrowth or hedgerows, especially in areas of low human traffic. Yet scent is their primary sense, as it is the most

Eurasian badger (top) with a North American badger misidentified as a 'Carcajou' (wolverine) below, from a 19th-century edition of Buffon's *Histoire naturelle*.

1. Le Blaireau. 2, Le Carcajou

Rendition of a Eurasian badger sett and surroundings by artist John Hicks.

functional for helping them to navigate the social and physical world of the subterranean habitat in which hearing and sight would be compromised. Indeed, their highly attuned sense of smell makes Eurasian badgers difficult to observe without discovery, as many eager but disappointed, dusk-crouching badger-watchers have learned.

In spite of its formidable predatory potential, the Eurasian badger as a species is nevertheless the most omnivorous of all mustelids, with various insects and larvae, small mammals, birds, reptiles, amphibians and freshwater invertebrates joining a diverse range of plant materials in its diet, including seeds, fruit, berries, roots and nuts. Earthworms are an important but variable food source: both field and post-mortem observation has confirmed that, given the right weather and habitat, a badger might consume

Eurasian badger snout.

hundreds of earthworms in a single feeding.[37] Its dietary preference for crop-raiding rodents and insects makes the Eurasian badger of significant benefit to farmers. Unfortunately, in part due to occasional crop depredations, damage to fields, lawns and fences from their burrowing activities and, more recently, the publicized panic about bovine tuberculosis, the species has been left with many enemies among farmers, winemakers and even urban gardeners.[38]

Eurasian badgers have also been implicated in the population decline of the hedgehog, another iconic and beloved UK species. This has recently become further rationale for the badger cull. But as Hugh Warwick points out, the two species are in an 'asymmetric intra-guild predatory relationship', in which both pursue the same food sources, largely earthworms. When access to adequate food is stable, badgers have little interest in hedgehogs, but 'when times are hard the relationship changes to one of predation'.[39] The issue, then, is less about getting rid of badgers than about making land management policies better for wildlife – a far more complicated and less politically expedient solution.

Mating is a late summer or early autumn activity and is sometimes accompanied by harrowing vocalizations that resemble human screams. In August 2008 police in Linz, Germany, responded with a helicopter search to concerned calls from residents about a woman being brutalized in a nearby wood. The discovery that the sounds were not 'a violent maniac and his terrified victim', but rather 'a number of romantically inclined badgers engaged in the pursuit of love' was both a relief and an embarrassment to the local constabulary.[40] Though a story that clearly amused international media commentators, the sound is far from humorous to those who have heard it. Indeed, the amorous call 'resembles the death scream of a mortally wounded badger, a sound which is so terrifying that many a hunter has ceased getting badgers after hitting one and hearing the cry'.[41]

In colder climes Eurasian badgers enter a winter torpor that may last a few months in the UK to up to six or more in Russia and the Scandinavian countries. During this 'indolent' time both male and female badgers subsist largely on their stored body fat in a state of drowsy lethargy. (Low body weight can be fatal during this period, as awakened badgers may starve if forced to forage in weather where dietary staples are unavailable.) Female

Eurasian badger family foraging.

badgers, like female bears, have the ability to delay implantation of fertilized eggs for long periods; depending on health, fat stores and weather conditions, egg implantation may be delayed for months during the winter torpor. In most conditions, births generally occur between January and March. Cubs are born with the trademark badge already in evidence; they emerge from the sett after weaning, generally between March and May. Litters average between two and four cubs, with only half that number typically surviving to their second winter.

The social life of Eurasian badgers extends even to their waste. Their use of specified seasonal latrines has been the focus of a great deal of scientific attention. Latrines are most prominent in defended territories with sizeable badger populations from different cetes; latrines can number in the dozens, and provide numerous useful functions. They are of practical hygienic use, since frequent defecation within the sett by multiple badgers (especially during mating and cub-rearing seasons) would soon render it uninhabitable. Latrines are also of territorial importance. Recent research indicates that cete members are quite deliberate in using latrines as boundary markers against outsider badgers, distributing faeces, urine and various glandular secretions in particular, non-random patterns.[42]

Although badgers, like most carnivores, can be fiercely territorial with those animals outside its social group, the Eurasian badger's reputation for general aggressiveness seems misplaced. Numerous accounts from researchers and interested observers challenge the stereotype of the belligerent badger. If anything, the picture that emerges is one of an engaging, tenacious, but largely shy and generally inoffensive omnivore that avoids interacting with humans as much as possible while pursuing its everyday activities.

The popular image of badger aggression in a 2002 *New Yorker* cartoon by C. Covert Darbyshire.

The Comte de Buffon's encyclopaedic and supposedly authoritative *Histoire naturelle* made him highly unpopular in the North American colonies. Particularly controversial was his unproven but oft-repeated assertion that American plants and animals were inferior in strength, size and virility in comparison with their European counterparts.[43] For the political and cultural leaders of the fledgling United States, such contemptuous Continental bias wrapped in scientific surety encouraged European doubts about the young nation's capabilities, and thus stood as a very real barrier to American hopes for foreign investment to rebuild and extend its own economy and influence.

Thomas Jefferson was a keen and internationally respected student of the natural sciences as well as a famous political figure. (His leisure to pursue these studies was largely provided by the African Americans enslaved on his Virginia plantation of Monticello, vital if often unacknowledged contributors to his

North American badger from *The Quadrupeds of North America*, by John James Audubon and Revd John Bachman (1852–4).

political and scientific legacies.) There was no prominent American better suited to respond forcefully and credibly to Buffon's insulting claims, and Jefferson engaged the great French naturalist with characteristic zeal, partially in patriotic defence of his homeland and partially out of wounded intellectual pride.

His *Notes on the State of Virginia* of 1785 is, in large part, a point-by-point challenge to Buffon's claims, arguing exactly the opposite, that North American animals (and the Indigenous peoples of the continent) were stronger and more robust than European species. Jefferson makes passing mention of badgers in his response to Buffon, but here his knowledge, like Buffon's, is incomplete. In the chart 'A Comparative View of the Quadrupeds of Europe and America', badgers are noted to be 'Aboriginals of both', but with no further details.[44] Later, Jefferson cites earlier observers with personal experience unavailable to either himself or Buffon:

> The weasel is larger in America than in Europe, as may be seen by comparing its dimensions as reported by Mons. D'Aubenton and Kalm. The latter tells us, that the lynx, badger, red fox, and flying squirrel, are the same in America as in Europe, by which expression I understand, they are the same in all material circumstances, in size as well as others: for if they were smaller, they would differ from the European.[45]

Jefferson, however, was wrong: the North American badger differs substantially from its European kin. He would not encounter more precise information about this creature and its distinctions from the Eurasian badger until 1803–5, when Meriwether Lewis and William Clark explored the Louisiana Purchase, the territorial claims that had been negotiated with France (but not, significantly, its Indigenous inhabitants) during

Jefferson's presidency. The journey was in large part a scientific expedition to study the flora and fauna of the American West. Clark records what may be the first encounter of English-speaking observers with a North American badger:

Joseph Fields Killed and brought in an Anamale Called by the French *Brárow* [*blaireau*], and by the Ponies [Pawnees] *Cho car tooch* this Anamale Burrows in the Ground and feeds on Flesh, (Prairie Dogs), Bugs, & vitatables – 'His Shape & Size is like that of a Beaver, his head mouth &c. is like a Dogs with Short Ears, his Tail and Hair like that of a Ground Hog, and longer, and lighter. his Internals like the internals of a *Hog*,['] his Skin thick and loose, his Belly is White and the Hair Short – a *white* Streek from his nose to his Sholders.[46]

Profile of North American badger (*Taxidea taxus*).

After being thoroughly examined by the curious travellers, the dead badger was skinned and stuffed for delivery to Jefferson. This pelt was likely 'the first zoological specimen preserved by Lewis ... We do know that before long, after the President had received the specimen, he informed a scientific friend that it was "not before known out of Europe" ... Apparently he knew nothing of specimens sent at any earlier date from Canada to Europe.'[47]

Nor did Jefferson seem to be familiar with the French *Codex Canadensis*, a compendium documenting about 1,700 of the animals and peoples of 'New France' encountered by the Jesuit missionary Louis Jordan (or even earlier Spanish colonial accounts).[48] (The manuscript remained unpublished until 1930.) Among the many creatures featured in Jordan's detailed ink sketches is perhaps the first European drawing of a North American badger, 'Le blereau': apart from its over-long tail, the image is easily identified as *Taxidea*, complete with distinctly striped pelage, powerful and stocky legs, and long, flattish body. Lewis and Clark's 'brárow', then, is a distinctively American species, one that would have provided a powerful challenge to Buffon's Eurocentric sense of environmental supremacy had Jefferson known of it twenty years earlier.

Although both species inhabit similar biological niches in their respective ecosystems, there are significant differences between the Eurasian and North American badgers, beyond even physical dissimilarities, as Scots-Canadian naturalist Ernest Thompson Seton observed in 1909:

Those who know the Badger of Europe have little idea of the life of the prairie species. The former seems to live much like a Skunk, trotting about at night, above ground, seeking its food in the woods and thickets, retiring to an underground home to rest during the hours of daylight.

Manitou ou nigani Enfant du P.31.
diable

18.

Le blereau

I

esseban ou attisonjou chat
sauuages 2

Le Glenard Blanc
3

THAT BADGERS SCRATCH AND BITE
IS GENERALLY SUPPOSED
BUT THIS IS NOT ONE TO FIGHT.
HE'D RATHER KISS YOU ON YOUR NOSE.

SWINNERTON
AUGUST-22-

Sketch in an Arizona guest ranch registry by cartoonist and landscape artist James (Jimmy) Swinnerton, 1922.

But the prairie Badger spends the greater part of its life underground, where it digs, feeds, sleeps, and multiplies much like a Mole. It rarely comes out during the day, except to bask in the sun by its doorway, and then is ready to plunge below at the slightest alarm.[49]

Habitat is certainly a difference: the Eurasian badger is found primarily in and around forests and woods, or in overgrown areas out of immediate human traffic, but its North American relative makes its home in fields, alpine meadows, open grasslands and deserts, and other spaces where soil is easily displaced to facilitate digging and predation.

The Latin-Greek *Taxidea* in Linnaean taxonomy firmly connects the North American badger with its Eurasian counterpart: *taxo* is the Latin root for badger, while *eidos* is the Greek word for 'type' or 'idea', thus *Taxidea* is roughly 'a type of badger', with the Eurasian species standing as the point of comparison. (The second part of its scientific name, *taxus*, is simply another medieval Latin term for badger.) Like all badgers, the North American species has numerous names among its long-time human neighbours. Among the Nahuatl speakers of northern Mexico, the badger is *tlalcoyotl*, meaning 'earth coyote' and gesturing to the frequent interactions between the two

'Le blereau', from Louis Nicolas's 17th-century *Codex Canadensis*, perhaps the first European depiction of a North American badger.

species. (In Mexico today the term often refers to an evil spirit rather than a live badger.) Among the Yoreme (or Mayo) of western Mexico, the term is *hú:ri*. The Keres-speaking Acoma Pueblo peoples of the southwestern U.S. call the animal *dyuupih*; the Diné (Navajos) say *nahashch'id*, for 'scratches around'; while in Hopi the word is *honani*, and its subject is greatly honoured in both story and ceremony. Among my Oklahoma Cherokee kin, the word is *uguna*; among the Lakotas of the central Great Plains, it is *hoka*. The Algonquian-speaking Potawatomi peoples say *msuguk*, and in one Anishinaabe dialect in Ontario, badger is *mishauk-waukidjeesh*. Among scientists there are four widely agreed upon subspecies of North American badgers, with populations largely stable in the U.S. but ranging from being of special concern to endangered throughout Canada and Mexico.[50] While habitat loss, traffic fatalities and killings by ranchers and hunters have negatively impacted many populations, other human activities have actually helped to facilitate slow recovery in some regions, especially when forested areas have been opened up for parkland, farming or ranch pasturage.

Physically, the North American badger has been described as 'very turtlelike, much as if someone took a half-grown European badger and then beat it until it was flat and broad'.[51] Smaller and wider than its Eurasian relative, with a less hunched profile and with a lower centre of gravity, though sharing its loose skin and rough fur, the North American species is sexually dimorphic (males and females differ in size, with females on average visibly smaller than males). Length ranges from 42 to 72 cm (16.5–28 in., excluding the short tail), while weight can vary from between 3.5 and 10 kg (roughly 8–22 lb).

The North American badger's 'badge' and head are quite distinctive from those of its Eurasian kin, even without comparing body profiles. The nose is sharper and less prominent on the North American badger, the ears larger and more pronounced,

the head wider and neck coat thicker and closer to the shoulders. While the body fur is more brownish-grey or silver than the grey-black of the Eurasian badger, it is the facial marking of *Taxidea* that is unique: the white stripe down the centre of the dark-furred forehead to the nasal bridge is narrow, stretching backwards to the end of the neck or, in the case of the Mexican subspecies, all the way down its body. White fur stands out by broadly surrounding the ears and extending across the side of the face to the eyes and muzzle, and the cheeks are marked by dark brown to black 'badges' surrounded by the white fur of the face, resembling side-burns. It is a more complex pattern than that of its Eurasian counterpart, but perhaps serves the same function: although the North American badger has better eyesight, the distinctive markings may help both species to identify other badgers at a distance and serve as a bold, recognizable warning to potential predators. The uniquely bold dorsal stripe of the Mexican subspecies may even

*The Political Badgers*, wood engraving by Mexican artist Leopoldo Méndez, 1944.

serve to disorientate aerial predators; given its notably smaller size compared to other badger subspecies, it would be in much more danger from eagle attacks, so such an adaptation would be a clear survival advantage.[52]

The North American badger has thick claws and slightly webbed feet, especially at the front. Combined with its tunnelling frame and musculature, protective nictitating membrane over its eyes and coarse guard hairs over its ears, and these claws, it has exceptional digging abilities. Of all the badgers, the North American species is perhaps the most powerful and effective burrower, having been observed not only to completely disappear through hardened soil in mere minutes, but even to systematically dismantle a concrete floor.[53]

Eurasian badgers live for long periods in complex and communal setts, but the more solitary North American badgers tend to make many (sometimes hundreds) of burrows of limited depth dispersed over an extensive territory that they occupy only briefly. Few burrows extend longer than 50 feet, and most are shorter given that they are generally used for a single night between late spring and late autumn, longer in the torpor-inducing winter. Badgers are innate recyclers, reusing not just their own burrows but also those of other badgers; such custom-made homes are also popular among other ground-dwelling wildlife, including rattlesnakes and burrowing owls. Territorial boundaries and badger densities vary depending on prey and mate availability, season and climatic conditions, ranging from 240 hectares (2.4 sq. km) to more than 50,000 ha (500 sq. km). The larger the territory, the greater the risk to the badger, especially in areas of high human population density and motor traffic.[54]

The North American badger is primarily (though not exclusively) carnivorous, preying mostly on small invertebrates and burrowing rodents. They are skilful and efficient predators of ground squirrels, marmots, prairie dogs, pocket gophers and other small mammals, along with birds, small reptiles, various amphibians and insects, and even rattlesnakes (like their distant honey badger kin, they seem to have some measure of venom resistance). There is also fascinating evidence that this species demonstrates rudimentary tool use when hunting Richardson's ground squirrels: one researcher observed a badger dragging soil, stones, wooden blocks, mud bricks and other objects to plug escape holes before beginning a focused dig.[55]

Mating takes place in the late summer or early autumn, and as with Eurasian badgers, implantation of the egg on the uterine wall is typically delayed until late winter to enable a spring birth. Litters of up to four offspring are comparable to those of their European kin, and kits (the preferred North American terminology) appear above ground to forage and learn to hunt with their mothers within a few months of birth. Although now a protected species in some Canadian provinces and u.s. states, badger kits were once a not-uncommon pet among both the poor and the

Archie Roosevelt,
son of President
Theodore
Roosevelt, with
Josiah, the White
House badger,
c. 1903–5.

wealthy, especially in the early twentieth century as the conservation movement became increasingly prominent.[56] The most famous of these pet badgers, Josiah, belonged to President Theodore Roosevelt, who received the kit from a schoolgirl while travelling through Kansas in 1903. Josiah joined a White House menagerie that at times included flying squirrels, kangaroo rats, a barn owl, a bear named Jonathan Edwards and even a hyena, and was a particular favourite of Roosevelt's fifth child, Archibald. The progressivist Roosevelt was so delighted by Josiah that he jokingly suggested starting his own Badger Party if the conservatives in his Republican party threw him out.[57]

Well known to be formidable foes to those threatening body, brood, food or territory, North American badgers have been observed to drive coyotes, dogs, foxes, and even immature cougars and bears from downed prey. Although the defensive spray of skunks is a deterrent to many potential predators, it is not much use against badgers, which can track prey through hearing as well as smell and vision. Not even frogs or other aquatic life are entirely safe from predation, as on rare occasions badgers have been known to swim.[58] Few animals have the tenacity to kill badgers, though hawks and eagles are dangers to kits, and coyotes, wolves and feral or domesticated dogs are a very real danger, especially in packs.

Yet, as is also the case with the Eurasian badger, the capacity of the North American badger to be aggressive in defence or fierce in hunting has led to an overblown emphasis on its supposed ferocity, which in reality is almost always defensive in nature. As the available scientific, anecdotal and experiential archive demonstrates, the reserved and curious North American badger is an intelligent, good-natured creature when left alone or treated with respect, but not one to accept malicious teasing or torment without fighting back.

Thus far we have given primary focus to the world's two most popular and widely studied species of badgers. Now we move to

North American badger in a defensive position.

61

a short discussion of the lesser-known but no less fascinating badgers: *Arctonyx*, the hog badger of southeast Asia, and *Mellivora*, the honey badger or ratel, the most physically distinctive member of the extended badger family, found throughout Africa, the Middle East and parts of India and Asia.

### *ARCTONYX*, THE HOG BADGER

European naturalists of the eighteenth and nineteenth centuries occasionally came across mention of another badger species somewhat unlike that of the more familiar Eurasian variety. Consistent with all taxonomic issues relating to badgers, the encounters caused no end of speculation and debate. Thomas Bewick provides a brief but intriguing account about 'The Sand-Bear' in his fourth edition of *A General History of Quadrupeds* (1800):

> We have given the figure of this animal, drawn from one kept in the Tower; of which we have not been able to obtain any further description, than its being somewhat less than

*Sand-bear*, or *Balisaur*, etching from Joseph B. Holder's *Animate Creation* (1885).

SAND-BEAR, OR BALISAUR.—*Arctonyx collaris.*

the Badger, almost without hair, extremely sensible of cold, and burrows in the ground. From these circumstances, as well as from the striking similarity of its figure to that of the Badger, we are inclined to think it is a variety of that animal, mentioned by naturalists under the name of the *Sow-Badger*.

Its colour is a yellowish-white: Its eyes are small; and its head thicker than that of the common Badger: Its legs are short; and on each foot there are four toes, armed with sharp white claws.

M. Brisson describes a white Badger, from New-York, so similar to this, that we suspect it to be the same species.[59]

Rather than the North American species, both the woodcut that accompanied the text and the description hint more toward *Arctonyx*, more commonly known today as the hog badger for its hairless, flexible, pig-like snout. The creature in the woodcut has a long tail, distinctive badged fur patterning and long claws, all characteristic features of the hog badger. *Arctonyx*, however, has a thick coat, so the hairlessness referred to by Bewick could have been due to inaccurate observation or reportage, a seasonal moulting, parasites or illness – the last being likely if the tropical animal was truly 'kept in the Tower' and was notably 'sensible of cold'. (The Tower of London was home to the Royal Menagerie until the 1830s and housed many exotic animals from across the world – living gifts to English royalty from foreign diplomats and visiting nobility that were largely ill-adapted to the climate and brutal conditions of English captivity.[60])

While known by many of its human neighbours in the modern states of Bangladesh, China, India, Indonesia, Laos, Malaysia, Thailand and Vietnam for far longer, it was in 1825 that the hog badger received its taxonomic classification from Europeans, given by Cuvier: *Arctonyx collaris*. (Again the historical link of badgers with bears is invoked by the name: *Arktos* is 'bear' in Greek, and thus the root of Arctic, in reference to the bear constellations Ursa Major and Ursa Minor, prominent in northern night skies but not in those of its opposite, the *Ant*arctic, a place without bears on the ground or in the stars.)

The local names of the hog badger tend to emphasize its resemblance to other creatures. According to some sources, the Hindi word for the hog badger (variously spelled *bahla-sur*, *balisaur* or *balizaur*) is rendered as 'bear pig' or 'sand hog', while the Burmese *Khwe-ta-wek-wek-ta-wek* or *Khwe-tu wet-tu* translates roughly as dog-pig.[61] A regional term in Guandong province, China, translates as 'dog bear'.[62] In body it certainly seems a strange synthesis of the now familiar trinity of badger, bear and pig, with dog thrown in for good measure. Similar in size to its Eurasian relative, the average length of the hog badger is around 70 cm (28 in.) plus a tail of 12 cm (4.5 in.) or more – the longest of all the badgers – with a weight of 14 kg (31 lb). Its front claws are long, curled and white, unlike those of the Eurasian badger, which are straighter

Hog badger
(*Arctonyx collaris*).

and darker. There is less fur contrast in the hog badger's markings than in its kin; although it shares the dark eye stripes and the white stripe from snout to nape, its shaggy fur varies in colour, with considerable subspecies variation from yellowish and brown to grey.[63] The second half of its taxonomic name – *collaris* – refers to the white collar of fur that stretches across the throat and over the ears, which is distinctive of this species.

Compared to its better-known badger counterparts, the life of the hog badger is rather mysterious. The available archive is sparse, due in part to the species' declining population throughout its range, with most zoological sources dated to the period of British imperial rule throughout much of its habitat and reflecting the particular cultural limits and biases of the chroniclers. A reclusive inhabitant of the tropical rain forest, the hog badger is, like *Meles*, a confirmed omnivore, with invertebrates, roots and small animals among its primary foods.[64] Its sense of smell is at least as good as that of the Eurasian badger. Similar to other badgers, its skin is tough and loose, affording significant protection from attack and injury, and its anal scent glands provide pungent supplemental defence. Like its relatives, it is fierce when threatened, though it is reportedly hunted for food by a number of larger predators, including tigers and humans.[65] Yet it is also said to be quite docile among humans, with reports of being 'so tame they come into villages and sleep among peoples' pigs'.[66]

The long claws are put to good use in burrowing for food and constructing birthing dens. Mating behaviour seems to be similar to that of its Eurasian relative, including delayed implantation. Litters range from one to four young, and mature size is reached by eight months.[67] There is debate among researchers about whether there are three species or one species and six to eight subspecies, with significant size and hair variation, although recent scholarship seems to support the former: the medium-sized *Arctonyx albogularis*, resident primarily in the Himalayas and throughout southern China; the largest and most common subspecies, *A. collaris*, which ranges throughout Southeast Asia; and *A. hoevenii*, the smallest of the group, found exclusively in the mountains of Sumatra.[68]

Much remains to be learned about the hog badger, its natural history, habits and lore. At present, due to its dropping numbers, reclusive nature and difficult home terrain, it remains the least understood of all the true badgers, and with further pressures on its population and habitat, time seems to be running out to learn more.

### *MELLIVORA*, THE HONEY BADGER OR RATEL

In July 2007 British troops stationed near the city of Basra in Iraq discovered that they were under scrutiny for what was rumoured to be a rather unconventional military action: the use of 'strange man-eating, bear-like' badgers to terrorize the urban population. After some of the feared creatures were killed and brought to local veterinary officials, it was announced that, rather than an introduced species of genetically modified monsters, the animals were, in fact, of a formidable but nonetheless quite natural neighbour species: the honey badger, or ratel, *Mellivora capensis*. According to officials, the badgers likely appeared in the city as a result of local habitat loss and associated prey disruption.[69]

Although the honey badger is native to the Middle East and throughout Africa, even as far as India and the Himalayas, it is hardly surprising that for many of the inhabitants of urban Basra this animal would seem entirely alien. Uncommon even at its greatest population density, and increasingly rare over much of its range, the honey badger is nocturnal and generally avoids humans. And like its distant badger brethren, the ratel is a creature

Joseph Wolf, *Ratels*, 1864, watercolour on paper.

more familiar through stories and stereotypes than through actual observation.

For those who have seen it in life, on film or online, honey badgers are unmistakable. With long, muscular bodies, they move on stout legs with a bowlegged trot, and their spade-like front claws are longer than those of their hind feet. They have shorter snouts and faces than Eurasian or hog badgers, even more so than North American badgers. A particular oddity is their lack of a visible external ear. In fact, the ear canal is fully functional and can be closed by interior muscles when the badger is digging or raiding beehives.[70] Like other badgers, its vision is comparatively poor and its sense of smell is dominant. Physically, the honey badger seems something like a hybrid creature with the body of a wolverine and the head of a docile sloth or pangolin – at least until it exposes its long, flesh-rending canines. Like its distant North American cousin, the heavily carnivorous ratel has fewer teeth than the more omnivorous Eurasian and hog badgers, meant primarily for ripping flesh, not chewing plant matter.

Roughly the size of the Eurasian badger, honey badgers vary in size according to sex, with the average male measuring 98 cm (38.5 in.) long, and females 91 cm (36 in.), with both sexes weighing roughly 9 kg (20 lb) each; African ratels are slightly larger than their Asian counterparts.

Perhaps the most distinctive feature of the honey badger is its wide dorsal stripe, which stretches from its forehead to the base of its shortish tail; the stripe itself is most often white or light grey, while the rest of the body is a dark grey, black or deep brown. The pattern appears shortly after birth and exhibits regional variation throughout the ten subspecies of the badger's wide range. The bold and flashy stripe serves as a warning, much like that of the skunk, and woe to the creature that disregards it.

Historically, the ratel has had a widely negative reputation. The idea of the Basra 'monster badger' is actually an extension of earlier prejudices, where the honey badger was called the *Garta* and featured in frightening stories for children.[71] Among the Asante people, the ratel is known as *sisi(ri)* or *kwabrafoɔ* – the latter related to *ɔbrafo*, which means 'executioner' – and they respect it as one of the strongest and most fearless creatures in their homeland.[72] Portrayed by many commentators as far more aggressive and unpredictable than carnivores of larger size, the honey badger is reputed to take down even African buffaloes through grisly genital mutilations (though researchers Colleen and Keith Begg are sceptical of this claim, as there have been no confirmed accounts of such behaviour since at least 1950 in spite of increasing research and field observation).[73] Among the Sindhi people of present-day Pakistan, the ratel is called *gorpat*, 'the gravedigger', for its rumoured proclivities for exhuming and eating human corpses; to Somalis, the bite of a ratel renders a man infertile.[74] It is reputed to be 'the most fearless animal in the world', as much for its supposed genital attacks as for its voracious appetite and willingness to attack anything that might be edible, including scorpions, cobras, adders and even young crocodiles.[75] (As discussed in more detail in chapter Three, the viral YouTube video mentioned earlier and subsequent marketing meme, 'The Crazy Nastyass Honey Badger', uses humour to capitalize on these sensationalized qualities.)

While some aspects of the ratel's fearsome reputation are exaggerated, there is little doubt that the honey badger is an effective predator of extraordinary tenacity and strength. Indeed, it seems that its fierceness is an ancestral trait that has impacted the evolutionary defences of one of its four-legged neighbours, the cheetah. Researchers have hypothesized that cheetahs have evolved a protective coat patterning among kittens to resemble that of an adult ratel, with a stripe of white fur on the back and darker fur elsewhere, so as to avoid predation by other carnivores. Whereas in many mammals their coat is intended to make them blend into the background and avoid detection from either predators or prey (a pattern called counter-shading), the honey badger's bold markings are an overt signal to others.[76] Indeed, the honey badger's 'very conspicuous colouring is correlated with its being virtually free from attack, an immunity it may owe partly to its possession of stink glands but is mainly due to its own physical power and a disposition that veers between fearlessness and unobtrusiveness'.[77] As few animals prey on the intimidating honey badger, the similarly sized cheetah kittens are protected through this mimicry at the stage when they are most vulnerable to sight-dependent carnivores and raptors.

The honey badger is fully equipped to challenge most antagonists. Sharing the long claws, sharp teeth and solid musculature of its badger kin, the ratel is also protected by its skin, which is 'exceptionally thick and tough' and 'loose so that [it] can twist enough to bite an attacker wherever it may grip'.[78] While it is not

Honey badgers facing down a pack of African wild dogs.

unheard of for honey badgers to fall prey to hyenas, lions, jackals, leopards, dogs, tigers and other solitary or pack predators, it is unusual; there are more reports of ratels, alone or in small groups, driving away much larger predators, both in self-defence and in conflict over food. It also has a remarkable (if not yet understood) ability to survive the effects of some of the most toxic snake venoms, a trait that seems to be shared to a lesser degree by North American badgers. The Beggs filmed one healthy young male killing a puff adder and suffering a bite that would have been fatal to a lion many times his size. Although his face swelled at the strike site and he contorted into what seemed to be an almost comatose state, within two hours he had fully returned to consciousness and, amazingly, finished eating the remnants of the adder.[79] And if poison resistance, thick skin, sharp teeth and dangerous claws were not enough, the ratel's notorious musking glands are capable of emitting an oily substance so intensely

70

pungent (colloquially called a stink bomb) that it has been reported to anaesthetize bees still in the hive during a honey raid.[80]

Like its North American counterpart, the honey badger is primarily carnivorous and given the opportunity it eats almost anything: a wide range of small mammals, young of larger animals, reptiles, birds, amphibians, invertebrates and, as is implied by its Sindhi name, even carrion. The food with which the ratel is most closely associated, however, is honey – the first part of its Latin name (and the English derivative) comes from the words *mel* (honey) and *voro* (to devour).[81] The Afrikaans term 'ratel' is of uncertain derivation, though it is most likely from the Dutch *raat*, for honeycomb (although an alternate theory holds that it is a reference to the rattling sound the creature makes when agitated).[82]

As with bears, the honey badger's thick skin and bristly pelage offer significant protection from bee stings. One of the most fascinating interspecies relationships in the animal world is associated with its pursuit of honey. There is an intriguing oral tradition and literature supporting the collaboration between the ratel and

Honey-loving ratels are persecuted by beekeepers throughout their range, although there are current conservation efforts to increase consumer demand for 'badger-safe' honey.

the honeyguide, a small bird that leads the honey badger to bee-hives with 'an unceasing chatter, described as the sound made by a partially filled box of matches shaken rapidly lengthwise'. Also known as an indicator bird, the honeyguide flies from tree to tree, leading the ratel towards the targeted hive, and after the badger has torn into the hive and had its fill, the bird feeds on beeswax, its primary food.[83] This behaviour has not gone unnoticed by the animals' human neighbours. In his lush modern bestiary, *The Book of Barely Imagined Beings*, journalist Caspar Henderson speculates that the mutually beneficial relationship between the honey badger and the honeyguide (as reflected in the linked names for the animals, *Kìrìphá-kò* and *Thik'ìlí-ko*, respectively) was a possible model for social cooperation, communication and even survival among the Hadza peoples of what is now Tanzania.[84]

Early European observers believed that honey was the ratel's sole sustenance, and while it is certainly a prized food, honey is in fact only a small part of its diet. Its predilection for honey (and bee larvae) has, however, resulted in its persecution by commercial and traditional beekeepers, with substantial population losses throughout its range as a result.[85] Yet it is not only beekeepers who kill honey badgers; farmers and ranchers, too, have targeted them for occasional depredations of livestock. These actions have a particularly negative impact on the ratel population given that females usually give birth to only one or two whelps a year, and natural mortality is high in its unforgiving habitats. Adding the pressure of human persecution to what is already a fragile repro-ductive process may mean extirpation across much of its traditional range.

Whereas the Eurasian and hog badgers are closely related, and the North American badger represents a distinctive lineage that diverged from the ancestral root before those of its counterparts, the honey badger stands alone in subfamily Mellivorinae as an example of convergent evolution, whereby biologically distinctive creatures in different habitats evolve similar traits and behaviours within their respective ecological niches. While resembling the mustelid wolverine in physique, the honey badger is far more like its distant badger kin in behaviour, predation patterns and activity cycle. For these reasons, it is included here among the 'true' badgers while the stink badgers and ferret badgers are not – a consequence of the ever-evolving considerations that continue to shape the category of 'badger' today.

MELLIVORA SIGNATA

A drawing of *Mellivora capensis signata*, the speckled ratel of Sierra Leone, 1909.

Henry Thomas
Aiken, *Badger
Catching*, 1820,
colour lithograph.

Chromolithograph
of a Eurasian
badger from
Richard Lydekker's
*Wildlife of the
World* (1916).

## 2  Rise of the Delvers: The Symbolic Badger

Cool from the sett and redolent
of his runs under the night,
the bogey of fern country broke cover in me
for what he is . . .
Seamus Heaney, 'Badgers'

Badgers are creatures of the underworld, chthonic denizens of earthen darkness. While they spend much of their hunting and foraging time in the open air, it is in hidden places under the night sky or in the twilight hours that they are most commonly to be found, not openly in the light of day. Otherwise, for most badger-kind, their cycles of life and death take place in the lightless world of sett and burrow. Symbolically, they inhabit the forbidden domain of the dead, the dangerous initiatory destination of culture heroes and ritualists who journey to the underworld in search of treasure, glory, knowledge or the departed spirits of loved ones. (Perhaps it is for this reason that the folkloric accounts of badger funerals are so evocative, as the idea that badgers engage in the practice of cere-monial burial has a long history in Europe. Most likely the practice is simply the hygienic disposal of deceased cete members into unused chambers that are then plugged to prevent the entire sett from being contaminated by the decaying body.)[1] Badgers thus inhabit a symbolic realm that humans can know only in ceremony and story, a liminal position between the dead and the living, the marvellous and the mundane. Small wonder, then, that badgers share both the mystery and the menace of these associations.

To some, they are magical creatures, guardians of the healing and protective secrets of the living earth. (This may be why the

Gaelic term for the priest-mystics of the ancient Picts was 'Brocan', for 'broc' or badger.[2]) To others, badgers are tenacious warriors, masters of metallurgy and the underworld's martial ways. While wolves, lions and bears might represent the military and political elite in iconography, the warrior-badger is fully one with the land and with those closest to it. Due to these elemental associations with the earth, they often represent tradition and stability, the fixed, conservative counterparts to the shape-shifting, rule-breaking fox or coyote. More recently, a third category of meaningful symbolism has emerged: that of 'spokesanimal', logo and corporate icon, where the badger's associations with natural living render it a useful advertising tool in an ecologically conscious era. In most of these cases, however, the symbolic badgers threaten to obscure the lives and struggles of the real animals themselves.

Take the u.s. state of Wisconsin as an example. Although the Eurasian badger is adored and despised with equal passion in the British Isles, there is no place in the world quite as badger-crazy as Wisconsin. Nicknamed 'the Badger State' (both for the North American species and for the lead miners who lived in

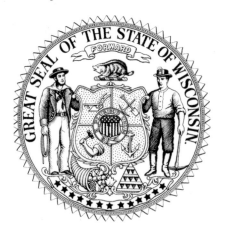

North American badger as crest animal in the official Great Seal of Wisconsin.

A gilded North American badger sits atop the head of the statue *Wisconsin* as it is raised onto the dome of the Wisconsin State Capitol, 1914.

burrow-like dugouts during the nineteenth century), it is a badger's paradise – at least in terms of symbolism.[3] *Taxidea taxus* is the state's official animal, and it stands statant (with all paws on the ground) as the crest figure of the state coat of arms; it is represented on the state flag and mentioned in the state song. There is even a bronze badger nestled among grapes on the gilded head of *Wisconsin*, a 3-ton allegorical statue standing atop the state

Once a popular Wisconsin roadside attraction, only the head and claws of the 'World's Largest Badger' remain today.

capitol building. The badger is everywhere in Wisconsin: on neon signs and coffee mugs, postcards and advertising flyers, and all manner of merchandise, as well as rather unusual architecture: the roof of a gift shop and filling station near Birnamwood was once adorned with a giant half-statue of the 'World's Largest Badger'. Yet for all their love of badgerish imagery and kitsch, most Wisconsinites, like the great majority of humans who live among badgers, have likely had little contact with the actual animals given their rarity in the state and nocturnal habits.

Nor does this seem to be a modern phenomenon. Badgers are only occasionally to be found in early pottery, rock paintings and pictographs, in which they seem to be roughly naturalistic, or where their symbolic significance is unknown. Rare in prehistoric and historical rock art, especially in comparison with the ritualistic hunting images of bison, wild cattle, deer and other large-hoofed prey, and often confused by modern viewers with bears and other animals of similar profile, identifiable badgers can nevertheless be found among the many carved animals and human-animal

78

hybrids. One of the more beautiful and recognizable Bronze Age images of a Eurasian badger is a Syrian terracotta figurine dating to between 2400 and 1900 BCE, which in 2004 sold with other artefacts at a Christie's auction for £478.[4] Honey badgers are quite rare in iconography, but one image in a rock shelter in what is now Bhopal, India, seems clearly to be a ratel, with elongated body, short muzzle and lack of visible ears.[5]

All badger species are inclined to be wary of humans. As represented in story, myth, legend, advertising, sport and war, however, badgers are anything but timid, being defined both by their link with the magic of the underworld and their largely undeserved reputation for innate aggression. These symbolic badgers are magicians, warriors, guardians and transformers, fierce mascots and cantankerous salesmen. Intriguing and often

*Tlalcoyote*, contemporary wood mask by Mexican artist Herminio Candelario Castro.

troubling constructs, they represent some of our most idealized characteristics, as well as some that are less endearing.

Most of the extant badger-themed petroglyphs and stone etchings in the rock art of the American Southwest are not as ancient as those noted above, dating roughly to the fourteenth and fifteenth centuries CE. Their meanings, however, while unclear to outside observers, have very clear significance in the ritual lives of the Indigenous peoples who continue to inhabit that region. The images generally focus on badgers' prominent clawed forepaws, but two in the Galisteo Basin near Santa Fe, New Mexico, represent full bodies in striking detail: one is a North American badger with massive curved claws extended, while the second seems to be a badger eating a snake.[6] In a northern Arizona site, the Hopi-style image of a badger has a medicine bundle on its back and a feather in its forepaw, indicating an ancient association with healing powers that continues today.[7]

Indeed, among many Native peoples of North America, the badger has long been a powerful being whose intimate familiarity

Badger petroglyph at Galisteo, near Santa Fe, New Mexico, c. 14th–15th century.

80

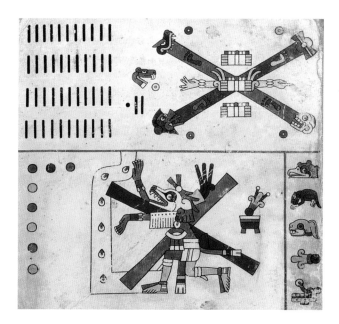

The Aztec god Xolotl, the Evening Star, at the crossroads of fate. From the *Codex Fejérváry-Mayer* (*Codex Tezcatlipoca*), painted on deerskin, c. 1200–1521 CE.

with the earth is reflected in his (or her) healing, transformational and divinatory gifts, and knowledge of the transitions of life and death. It is therefore likely that most relevant rock art images are associated with these traits, especially in the prairie and desert regions of the continent where badgers continue to be honoured in Indigenous traditions. Beyond rock art, some representations are clearly badgers, while others are more obscure but no less intriguing. The Aztec deity Xolotl, the Evening Star and misshapen brother of the more celebrated Quetzalcoatl, serves as occasional psychopomp for the spirits of the dead and guardian of the sun on its journey through the Aztec underworld of Mictlan. In surviving codices and statuary, Xolotl often wears what seems to be the head of a scavenging dog (a species also associated with death and the underworld in Aztec tradition), but some images seem more clearly to reflect the distinctive markings of the small Mexican badger, *T. t. berlandieri*.[8]

These traditional associations continue today. Among the Pikuni (Blackfoot) peoples of the prairies, the badger is an animal chief of particular significance. In one account, after a man's family is saved from starvation by a group of powerful animal beings, he is invited to enjoy the hospitality of some of the other carnivores but is warned to ignore the requests to visit by Skunk and Badger due to their foul odour. Eventually the man thinks better of ignoring Badger Chief's generous invitation and enters the lodge of the dignified animal, where Badger gives the man and his family a new lodge 'and the sacred songs that belonged to it'. Big Wolf later tells the man that Badger is 'the most powerful of us all'.[9] (Such power extends well beyond life, as badger entrails have historically been used for divination in Blackfoot ceremony.[10])

To the Cheyennes, Badger is one of the Maiyun (sacred beings); he is one of 'The Listeners Under the Ground', particularly respected 'because he possesses power to foretell the future'.[11] The Sioux nations have stories about Badger helping to create the first human, most often from a clot of bison blood. Badger's innate familiarity with nature's pharmacopoeia makes him particularly well suited for teaching about medicine. A Teton Sioux medicine man, Eagle Shield, attributed the medicine he used for children to a badger's dream visitations (interestingly, and consistent with other badger-bear connections, his medicine for adults was of the bear variety):

A man appeared to me in a dream, showed me a plant, and said, 'My friend, remember this plant well. Be sure to get the right one, as this is good.' It was a badger who appeared to me in the form of a man and said this. It was the first time that the badger came to me, but afterwards he brought me other herbs. There were no songs with any of the herbs which the badger brought me . . . Whatever herb the badger introduces is especially good. Some consider his medicine stronger than that of the bear, as he digs deeper and farther into the ground.[12]

Among the Arapahos, earth-growing medicines belong to Badger, who is gifted in their healing uses.[13]

In the traditions of the Pueblo peoples of the desert Southwest, Badger helped humans and all animals reach the current world from a previous one by digging through the rock wall or roof that separated the worlds.[14] Badger is also a great medicine person, and the Hopi Badger clan is tasked in part with the care of the kachina rituals and ceremonial calendar.[15] Indeed, Badger is a

Pueblo Indian badger katsina doll made for the collecting market, c. 2002.

83

prominent figure in Hopi stories; he is sometimes the target of Coyote's stratagems, but he has power and cunning all his own. He also has the power to raise the dead. In one version of the tale, when he and Coyote discover a young woman's corpse, Coyote begs his friend to use his medicine powers to resurrect her. Badger does so, but Coyote undermines the sanctity of the process through various disrespectful acts: first, he continually violates the privacy required by the ceremony; then he attempts to have sex with the newly revived woman and accidentally kills her in the process; finally, in spite of his friend's righteous anger, he refuses to honour the privacy Badger expects when the latter finally buries the twice-dead woman's body. The story ends with Old Man Badger eating Coyote as consequence for the latter's brutality, foolishness and greed.[16]

It is not just the dead that Badger has the power to revive: it is also flagging sexual potency. Among Hopis and other Pueblo peoples, he is at once diagnostician and healer of sexual dysfunction and impotence, sex therapist and epidemiologist able to identify even unusual sexually transmitted infections and assess their cures. (Further highlighting the association of Badger with the mysteries of human reproductive biology, badger medicine is also drawn upon for women in childbirth, though seemingly to a lesser degree.) It is Badger's 'stiffening medicine' that is the origin of the perpetual erection of the hunchbacked flute-player Kokopelli, an honoured fertility being whose appropriated image is castrated in the popular decals of Southwest desert-themed design.[17]

Contemporary Pueblo tradition is hardly alone in associating badgers and their various body parts with human virility and sexuality. This connection extends across continents and eras, going back hundreds of years. In a Middle English translation of the *Medicina de quadrupedibus*, a compendium of animal cures

84

and medicinal formulae, it is said that, if 'anything of evil has been done to any one so that he may not enjoy his sexual lusts, let him boil a badger's testicles in running spring-water and in honey and let him take it then fasting for three days; he will soon be better.'[18] A painting from the Italian Renaissance by the controversial painter Giovanni Bazzi (known generally as Sodoma – 'The Sodomite' – for his reputed sexual proclivities), is similarly intriguing in this regard. Two Eurasian badgers from his extensive private menagerie are featured next to his self-portrait, painted in the early 1500s as part of a fresco cycle of the *Life of St Benedict* at Monte Oliveto Maggiore in Tuscany. The animals stand at his feet, one collared and looking to the faded raven near the artist's right heel, the other looking up in devotion, or even in a manner that is less than spiritual. Perhaps Sodoma is having a cheeky sexual joke on the viewer, given that the unbound badger is peering up at the artist's genital area while Sodoma's visage sports a wry and knowing smile; certainly this would not have been out of character for the notoriously provocative artist.[19] Another century removed, Dr John Johnston assures readers in *A Description of*

The artist Sodoma included a self-portrait with two pet badgers in this religious fresco in the abbey of Monte Oliveto Maggiore. Detail from *The Life of St Benedict, Scene 3,* c. 1505–8.

*the Nature of Four-footed Beasts* (1678) that badger fat 'helps chapped nipples, and gouts, and shrunk-members'.[20]

The link between badgers, genitalia and sex can be found in both U.S. and UK slang even today, although unlike the Pueblo traditions noted above, these are generally with negative connotations. Derogatory or at least ambivalent uses of 'badger' refer variously to the vagina, an unattractive but sexually available older woman (distinguished from the more desirable 'cougar'), a man of any orientation obsessed with anal sex (thus the 'arse-badger' in England), a mercenary prostitute or blackmailer (sometimes accompanied by a thug ready to rob or extort the unsuspecting customer), a gay man looking for outdoor sex, and even a chamber-pot (with 'pulling the badger' the nasty trick of inviting a man to a badger-baiting and instead upending the chamber pot on him).[21] Perhaps the pungent gland secretions from the badger's nether-regions are linked to this association; certainly a number of current slang terms connect concepts of dirt and disgust with badgers and taboo sex.[22]

Badgers are associated with other powers beyond the sexual, having also served as astronomers, meteorologists and weather diviners to a number of cultures. While seemingly incongruent with traditional subterranean associations, their connections with darkness and distinctive pelage make them evocative celestial symbols, too. For example, there is an Apache story of Badger keeping all the world's darkness in a bag; ever-curious and ever-greedy Coyote opens the bag in hope of food and darkness is set loose forever. Similarly, the Mexican badger's long white stripe intersecting its speckled dark fur may have served historically as a physical metaphor for the Milky Way at night.[23] The North American tradition of Groundhog Day, whereby a groundhog is observed when it emerges from its burrow on 2 February, has its origins in German Candlemas celebrations involving a badger (or even a bear) as a predictor of winter's duration and the potential for a good harvest to come. If, when emerging from its burrow, the badger sees its shadow, winter will continue for six weeks; if not, an early spring is anticipated. Eighteenth-century German immigrants to Pennsylvania, finding no familiar Eurasian badgers in their new homeland (and far from the home range of the North American badger), adopted the local hibernating groundhog for the same purpose.[24]

A somewhat obscure area of the mystical and magical symbolism of badgers is in New Age and Pagan circles. Many contemporary Pagans combine earthen spirituality with rigorous scholarship, cross-cultural respect and careful observation about the other-than-human world.[25] Most mainstream writings that refer to 'badger medicine', however, are of the New Age self-help variety and tend towards romanticized excess, stereotyped and over-generalized claims, a sizeable amount of cultural and spiritual appropriation, and consistent confusion about the basic anatomical, habitat and behavioural differences between the Eurasian and North American species. Typically, badgers are listed as one of many generic animal 'spirit guides', 'familiars', 'allies' or 'totems', occasionally accompanied by animal-themed divination cards, and discussion is limited to a few superficial observations on the badger's earthy symbolism, as in the following representative sample:

> The badger is bold and ferocious, and it never surrenders. If a badger has come into your life, you should do some examination. Are you or those around you not digging deep enough? It may indicate a need to get beneath the surface. It may reflect a time of greater connection to the earth and its animal spirits.[26]

For all their vague generalizations and occasional cynical commercialism, these texts nevertheless respond to a widespread hunger for a closer connection with the other-than-human world. And as urbanization continues to impinge on the wild places of the earth and romantic nostalgia replaces lived experience, the increasingly lucrative market for 'power animals' will no doubt grow as well.

We cannot depart from a discussion about badger magic without mentioning the shape-shifting Japanese *tanuki*, which has long been associated with the badger in Western writings. Though the term *tanuki* has historically been used by non-Japanese to refer to the country's pale, brownish domestic badger, another word – *anaguma* (thus the taxonomic *Meles anakuma*) – specifically refers to badgers, with *tanuki* more accurately the name of the indigenous raccoon dog.[27] The subject of one folktale, 'Bunbuku Chagama', about a wondrous *tanuki*-spirit who transforms into a tea kettle and back again depending on how well he is treated by his various human companions, is frequently referred to by Western folklorists and commentators as a badger. Yet in historical and contemporary visual representations of the story, the figure

A *tanuki*-spirit sits in contemplation in Tsukioka Yoshitoshi's *Bunbuku chagama* (*The Clothes-changing Tea Pot*), c. 1889–92, woodcut.

is almost invariably a raccoon dog.[28] Another term, *mujina*, though sometimes referring to biological badgers, is generally associated with a spirit in badger form.[29] The distinctions between these various terms was significant enough to feature in a 1924 case before the Supreme Court of Japan, in which a man was acquitted of illegally hunting badgers, as in his community '*tanuki* were different animals from the badgers they called *mujina*', and the law in question regulated only the seasonal hunting of *tanuki*.[30]

Yet the badger and the raccoon dog still seem to be conflated in different regions of Japan, and for good reason, as both are somewhat similar in body and habit, being nocturnal and boldly marked omnivores largely unfamiliar to most humans, though the facial features of *tanuki* sculptures are quite clearly more reflective of the raccoon dog than the badger. They also feature similarly in folk tradition and ghost stories as shape-shifters, tricksters and transformer spirits who use their powers to beguile and manipulate their human neighbours. A popular contemporary children's rhyme indicates the *tanuki*'s generally benign character,

Raccoon dog, or *tanuki*.

Ohara Mitsuhiro,
*Badger Teakettle*,
mid-19th century,
ebony and metal.

thereby distinguishing it from the rather more malevolent *kitsune* fox-spirit of other tales and songs:

*Genkotsu-yama no Tanuki-san*
*Oppai nonde, nene shite*
*Dakkoshite*
*Ombushite*
*Mata ashi-ta!*

The little *tanuki* from Genkotsu mountain
nursing (him/her)self to sleep
carried in (mother's) arms
then piggy-backed
See you tomorrow![31]

A final note on *tanuki*'s possible badgerish connection: one of the more prominent features of smiling *tanuki* artworks is the giant scrotum that dangles to the floor between the potbellied figure's feet. Such genital excess would seem in keeping with badger lore elsewhere, and thus complicates what is already the rather tangled issue of badger nomenclature in Japan.

Badgers are not only represented as medicine keepers, mystics, or trickster-transformers – they are also warriors. Indeed, the original Gaulish root of today's brock may have meant 'point', in a nod to its spear- or arrow-shaped head.[32] Given their capacity for determined self-defence when tormented by human baiters and dog packs, badgers have long been associated with martial symbolism, though less prominently than larger carnivores or birds of prey. In many ways, badgers are creatures more suited to earthy images of modest, dependable and everyday valour than grand heraldic beasts, such as the regal lion and imperial eagle. These martial badgers are rarely idealized or romantic. Rather, they are stalwart, loyal and brave, and their representations often reflect such earthy concerns. Indeed, so practical are these associations that in Zambia the noses, hearts and tails of the injury-resistant honey badger are important to traditional medicine, ingested with other compounds to provide particularly good defence against stab wounds.[33]

There are various forms of weaponry that invoke badgers in both name and function, especially in the u.s. None is grand or ornate; all are quite utilitarian and devastatingly efficient. On the more mundane end, James Calhoon Manufacturing advertises the Badger, a .19 calibre 'varmint cartridge' intended specifically for killing small game such as prairie dogs, ground squirrels and even badgers.[34] Numerous American knife manufacturers advertise a Badger brand among their offerings. More dramatically, of the eleven u.s. nuclear bomb tests of Operation Upshot-Knothole, the only one to be named for an animal was Badger, detonated on 18 April 1953. Neither the most destructive nor powerful of the tests, Badger nevertheless offered something distinctive. True to the reputation of its wilful namesake, the Badger nuclear cloud shifted from its anticipated direction and exposed Marines to excessive levels of radiation as it drifted towards the Grand Canyon.[35]

Perhaps surprisingly, the earth-bound badger finds emblematic military service from sea to sky. At least eight British warships in the service of the Crown have carried the name of Badger. Horatio Nelson's first captaincy was of HMS *Badger* in 1777; the brig served in the Royal Navy until 1782. Of the three ships in the U.S. Navy commissioned under the name of USS *Badger*, only one was named for the animal; the other two were named in honour of prominent naval officers whose family name was Badger.

The NATO codename for the Tupolev Tu-16, one of the most successful bombers in the Soviet aerial arsenal, was Badger. It featured prominently in both military and civilian air travel from the start of its production in 1953 until around 1994. (In keeping with the now-familiar historical connection, a later and more imposing Tupolev aircraft, the Tu-95, was codenamed Bear.) The Tu-16 was an adaptable twin-engine aircraft and was frequently modified and retrofitted for different purposes during and after the Cold War, for medium-range theatre conflict to longer-range bombing missions, reconnaissance and even civilian transport. The Soviets exported the aircraft to its allies from the 1950s onward.[36]

The honey badger shares its Afrikaans name with the wheeled Ratel IFV (infantry fighting vehicle), the flagship combat vehicle of the South African National Defence Force. Originally designed and manufactured in South Africa to circumvent the effects of the anti-apartheid arms embargos, the Ratel-20 was heavily deployed in the country's conflict with Angola in the 1970s and '80s and continues to see service as an armoured personnel transport. In the U.S., as with other iconography of the Badger State, the North American badger serves as a symbol of fighting determination

South African Ratel infantry vehicle.

throughout the Wisconsin Air and Army National Guard, from the snarling North American badger head on the standard uniform patch and, for the last six years of its publication, the masthead of the *BAM* (for Badger Air Militia), the base paper of the 115th Fighter Wing, to actual deployments and operations, such as the 724th Engineer Battalion's Task Force Badger in Iraq.[37]

Not far removed from the world of military valour is that of sport, and the gap between badgers as martial symbols to mascots of sports teams is a narrow one. For both, badgers are invoked as idealized opponents, unyielding in the face of danger. Apart from crusty old Mr Badger of *The Wind in the Willows*, the most famous badger in the U.S. – or at least the one most prominent in merchandise and marketing – is likely Buckingham U. Badger (Bucky for short), the official mascot of the University of Wisconsin. A pugnacious North American badger in a white and red striped sweater with a large 'W' on the front, Bucky has become one of the most recognizable mascots in American university sports and easily the most beloved representative of the state. The earliest UW mascot was a live badger, but it proved to be both uncooperative and escape-prone. A captive raccoon served as mascot for a short while – Regdab ('badger' backwards), ostensibly a 'badger in a raccoon coat' – but it was ultimately exchanged on the field for a man in a badger costume.[38] Named in a school contest in the 1940s (replacing rather less exalted names such as Benny, Bernie and Bouncey), young men dressed as a smiling Bucky rally school spirit and 'fly the fur' at all Wisconsin Badgers games and hundreds of non-sporting events every year.[39]

Buckminster (Bucky) Badger, mascot of the University of Wisconsin.

Bucky's game-ready visage is featured on a wide range of paraphernalia and sports gear, including T-shirts, pens, hats, ornaments, car accessories, pet-ware and children's books. He was the focus of a 2009 documentary film, *Being Bucky*, which follows the experiences and personal challenges of some of the men who wear the costume.[40] And in addition to being a world-renowned symbol of the university and its numerous sports teams, Bucky is a lucrative source of revenue: since registering the mascot's image with the u.s. Patent and Trademark Office in 1990, the University of Wisconsin has benefited from millions of dollars in licensing royalties.[41] The Wisconsin National Guard has even nicknamed the badger that appears on their patch 'Bucky' in respectful honour of their state's most famous fictional resident.[42]

A more ferocious but less famous badger sport mascot is Boomer the Badger of the significantly smaller Brock University in southern Ontario. Badgers are not, however, the immediate genesis of the school's moniker, being a perilously endangered species in the province. Rather, Brock University was named for Sir Isaac Brock, who led British forces against the United States during the war of 1812 and died in the conflict. Curiously, while Boomer is quite clearly represented by the athletics department as a snarling North American badger, it is a demure and dignified Eurasian badger that stands as a supporter on the university's official coat of arms (not surprising considering that Canadian arms were granted by the uk College of Arms until the Canadian Heraldic Authority was created in 1988).

Badgers in heraldry:

The author's Canadian coat of arms, with a North American badger as the crest figure.

A Eurasian badger supporter represents Sir Isaac Brock, the namesake of Brock University.

The badger was chosen as a supporter in the corporate arms of hotelier The Bonnington Group, Ltd, due to its home-making associations.

As a bridge between badgers as martial symbols to those of more esoteric significance, heraldic representations are worth considering. Although cultures worldwide and throughout history have detailed protocols for choosing specialized symbols to represent individuals and particular genealogies (such as Haida hereditary crests and the Japanese *mon*), heraldry as we recognize it today has its primary origins in European chivalric tournaments and battle. The iconography of armorial achievements developed as a way of quickly identifying specific knights whose features were hidden from view by protective helmets.[43] (As discussed in chapter One, the knight's unique armorial badge is likely the origin of the English term 'badger'.)

Badgers are uncommon heraldic devices, though they make occasional appearances in European, Canadian and South African personal, corporate and municipal coats of arms, as well as in U.S. military heraldry. Given the longer history and greater prevalence of armorial achievements in Europe, it is no surprise that the Eurasian badger is the most common species to be represented in heraldry, and primarily, though not exclusively, in the UK, where they are most heavily invested with cultural meaning. But not all such meanings have endured to the present. In a seventeenth-century English armorial, among their various associations badgers are deemed symbolically 'Rapacious' and therefore categorized with 'Dog kind', along with dogs, wolves and foxes.[44] Similarly, while some of his contemporaries claimed that to 'bear the *Badger* or *Brock* is in memory of some stratagem performed in the night', the seventeenth-century heraldic artist Sylvanus Morgan supported the more mundane reference to 'the delight the Bearers had in hunting of the *Badger*'.[45] Most heraldic uses play with badger names, chiefly 'brock'. Prominent individuals with badger or badger-themed devices on their armorial bearings include the British diplomat John Anthony Sankey and Ralph Brocklebank, Fellow of both the Royal Heraldry Society of Canada and the Heraldry Society of the United Kingdom.

A number of municipalities include the Eurasian badger as crest figures atop or supporters on the side of the heraldic shield, including the Township of Brock in Ontario (whose crest features a brock that looks decidedly wolfish), the more geographically accurate Eurasian badger crest figures of the boroughs of Broxtowe, near Nottingham, and Broxbourne, and the badger supporter on the coat of arms of the former Municipal Borough of Sale (today part of Trafford in Manchester). Dachsbach ('badger-brook'), Germany, features a badger on its official shield, as does the Swiss community of Chabrey.

Businesses, too, occasionally feature badgers on their coats of arms: for example, the London-based Bonnington Group of hoteliers has a golden Eurasian badger supporter bearing a flaming torch as part of its armorial achievements. Along with its fellow supporter, a golden beaver, and a red elephant crest figure, it represents 'home-making skills in diverse habitats, which allude to the diversity of the company both in geography and in people', with the badger thus representing a transnational British industriousness.[46] In 2012 the British supermarket chain Tesco came under fire from animal rights activists for its support of pro-cull farmers. Protesters were quick to accuse the chain of hypocrisy given that its corporate coat of arms features not one but three Eurasian badgers.

### THE MARKETING BADGER

Indeed, it is in commercial representations that badgers most commonly abound, far out of proportion to their actual numbers, and often in ways seemingly disconnected from either their biology or their historical depictions. Restaurants, pubs, gift shops, filling stations, marketing agencies and numerous tea rooms in the UK and across North America prominently display badgers as advertising logos and mascots. Frontier Airlines of the U.S., which features full-colour animal photos on the tails of their aeroplane fleet, added a badger to a regional Embraer 190 aircraft in 2010, along with a naming contest for Wisconsin residents. 'Buddy the Badger' joined Montana the Elk, Grizwald the Grizzly Bear and Flip the Bottle-nosed Dolphin as one of more than 60 official 'spokesanimals' for the company.[47]

Badger-themed products are also popular and they often draw on the elemental associations of badgers with earthy naturalness. In New Hampshire the W. S. Badger Company, which manufactures dozens of organic, badger-themed skin care products, including Badger Balm – 'a simple, all-natural, soothing and healing balm that really work[s]' – has brought the smiling visage of a chubby North American badger into organic health stores throughout the U.S. and Canada.[48] In Dorset, on the other hand, the somewhat less health-conscious Hall & Woodhouse's Badger Brewery offers ales named after hares and ferrets as well as their trademark and award-winning Eurasian badger-themed beer, Badger First Gold.

The most recognizable Eurasian badger in advertising is likely that of the Badger Trust, Britain's badger protection and advocacy group. Its logo and other print ads keep the species and its welfare constantly in the public eye. Even for the majority of UK residents who have never encountered a living badger, the Trust's activism against repeated governmental and farm lobby calls for badger culls have brought the Trust to international attention. In Canada the most widely observed commercial badger is likely that on the equipment of the transnational Badger Daylighting – appropriately

enough, an excavation and trenching corporation often found on Canadian construction sites.

Badgers are hardly household figures in the mainstream U.S. media, but a badger in a regional advertising campaign became what one commentator called 'a viral marketing triumph', at least for a short time.[49] In Raleigh, North Carolina, the Martin Agency produced a series of humorous television commercials for Johnson Automotive that featured a North American badger puppet named Grady, a tacky car salesman with a gravelly southern twang who harangued potential customers at a dealership named, appropriately enough, Rankle & Chafe.[50] Grady epitomized all of the worst stereotypes about high-pressure salesmen, everything that Johnson assured its customers that its own sales employees are not with the taglines 'Tired of being badgered?' and 'Great deals. Great service. No badgers'.[51] Appearances on YouTube and other social media made him so popular that for a while Johnson Automotive set up a website (now defunct) to sell 'Badger Gear', including a talking Grady doll complete with hideous sport coat and trademark catchphrases.[52]

The most popular marketing badger of recent years, however, is 2011's viral YouTube video-turned-meme, 'The Crazy Nastyass Honey Badger'.[53] Featuring footage cut from a National Geographic documentary special with added voiceover commentary by flamboyant animal rights activist 'Randall' (likely the well-guarded alter ego of improv performer and writer Christopher Gordon), the video received more than 13 million hits in its first seven months online and was profiled by the *Huffington Post* and Forbes.com.[54] The video shows the honey badger capturing and devouring a variety of food, all described as 'disgusting' or 'nasty', and finally confronting, being poisoned by, and prevailing over a puff adder (which Randall identifies as a cobra, but this is due to the splicing together of the ratel's confrontation with two different snakes). Though 'Randall's Wild Wild World of Animals' features campy nature videos of animals as diverse as 'The Slowass Sloth' and 'The Gross and Disgusting American Bullfrog', along with more serious animal rights advocacy, it is the honey badger that has captured viewers' primary interest and financial investment. Others have capitalized on the video's popularity, and there is now an entire cottage industry of honey badger merchandise, including T-shirts, mugs, underwear, calendars, books, bumper stickers, posters and talking stuffed toys, as well as official Randall-approved iPhone apps featuring variations on the video's most memorable

Guy and Rodd,
*Honey Badger
Do Care*, 2012.

taglines, including 'honey badger don't care'. At the time of writing there is even a television show in development, tentatively titled *Honey Badger U*. The proposed show focuses on Randall as an animated science instructor who works at a university with, yes, a honey badger as its mascot.[55]

We have thus far explored the diverse spiritual and social symbolism of badgers; now we will examine how that symbolism plays out in artistic representations, especially those of art, literature, film and television. In so doing, we will consider what these imagined beings reveal about not only the history of the badger–human relationship, but its long-term possibilities.

# 3 Notable Badgers of Page and Screen

> 'I would ask you to remember only this one thing', said Badger. 'The stories people tell have a way of taking care of them. If stories come to you, care for them. And learn to give them away where they are needed. Sometimes a person needs a story more than food to stay alive. That is why we put these stories in each other's memory. This is how people care for themselves. One day you will be good storytellers. Never forget these obligations.'
>
> Barry Lopez, *Crow and Weasel* (1990)

Given the diverse symbolic representations of badgers, it is no surprise that literature, film and other arts reflect these often-contradictory attitudes, ranging from the ennobled paragon to the feral brute. Foxes, wolves, lions and other romanticized carnivores are more commonplace, but badgers are not strangers to the arts and popular culture. Some of these characters are complex and multidimensional, while others are more simplistic projections of our presumed virtues or, more rarely, vices. Very often they continue the tradition of the wise wilderness sage, although occasionally there are ignorant, cruel and even murderous badgers to be found. And as new technologies emerge, we can be certain that badgers will find a place there, too, though likely one that has more to do with our prejudices than with our experiences of badgers themselves. This chapter will consider some of the more evocative badgers of literature, film and other imaginative arts.

Although Eurasian badgers range from the Atlantic to the Pacific and nearly to the Arctic, there are comparatively few found in Chinese visual and literary arts, where the bear, lion, tiger and even dog feature far more prominently; badgers are similarly rare in Russian imagery. As discussed in the previous chapter, in Japanese folklore and art badgers are often conflated with raccoon dogs in stories and terminology, although the distinctions hold more clearly depending on region. So in this chapter we look mostly to the UK, Europe and North America for the most extensive archive of badger representations. And of those figures, one badger's shadow looms largest, influencing generations of readers and writers alike. Though not the first literary badger, he is undoubtedly the most famous, a certain genteel and earthy elder who abides in the pastoral past of another England that never was: Mr Badger, in Kenneth Grahame's beloved classic *The Wind in the Willows* (1908).

## BADGER OF THE WILD WOOD

Mr Badger embodies many of the symbolic characteristics of European badger lore and serves as a template for many that have followed on page and screen, being at once a woodland wise man, a suitably shabby bourgeois gentleman, a loyal companion, a stalwart and somewhat reactionary defender of old-fashioned social values, and a skilled fighter who challenges chaos with force when reason and conventional mores are no longer effective. To Water Rat, Mole and Toad, the other respectable beasts of the novel, he is friend and adviser; to the weasels, stoats and other mustelid riffraff of the Wild Wood, he is at best a standoffish neighbour, at worst an implacable foe. (Badger and Otter are the only weasel-kin represented as having distinctly noble qualities, as most of the others in the novel are brutes and boors.) Badger is the voice of history, tradition and the power of the land itself. Consider his words as he gives Mole a tour of his vast underground home built among the remnants of an ancient human city:

'But what has become of them all?' asked the Mole.

'Who can tell?' said the Badger. 'People come – they stay for a while, they flourish, they build – and they go. It is their way. But we remain. There were badgers here, I've been told, long before that same city ever came to be. And now there are badgers here again. We are an enduring lot, and we may move out for a time, but we wait, and are patient, and back we come. And so it will ever be.'[1]

Badger leads the liberation of Toad Hall, illustration by Ernest Shepard, 1931 edition of *The Wind in the Willows*.

Badger follows with a natural history of the Wild Wood as it reclaimed the land where once the human city had stood: 'the strong winds and persistent rains took the matter in hand, patiently, ceaselessly, year after year . . . Leaf-mould rose and obliterated, streams in their winter freshets brought sand and soil to clog and to cover, and in course of time our home was ready for us again, and we moved in.'[2]

Grahame was certainly not writing a zoological treatise in *The Wind in the Willows*; he was invoking a nostalgic Arcadia, 'a golden age of his own imagining . . . a Wild Wood that really threatens no evil, and a Wide World that one need never bother about at all'.[3] It is a setting of eternal adolescence, an unencumbered bachelorhood that is largely free of real menace or real responsibility (and which was far removed from Grahame's own unhappy personal life). It is also a male-dominated world where gender is largely fluid, and where the main characters are defined far more by their domestic delights and affections than with the very brief battle at the story's end.[4] The predatory behaviour of actual badgers is fully transformed by these social affiliations and rituals: in reality, toads, moles and water rats (or, more properly, water voles) would all be quick prey to Eurasian badgers, and Mr Badger's solitary life would be unusual indeed for a generally social species.[5] Yet other moments in the text reflect Grahame's careful observations of nature, such as Badger's refusal to confront Toad about his irresponsible behaviour until after his own winter torpor has passed, and the descriptions of the habits and habitations of the various beast-people who inhabit this gentrified world.

Old Badger's voice of tradition is not just that of badger history, but of class-conscious Edwardian society, as in his intervention when Toad's financial extravagance and wild driving bring disrepute on *all* the animal-folk:

'You knew it must come to this, sooner or later, Toad', the Badger explained severely. 'You've disregarded all the warnings we've given you, you've gone on squandering the money your father left you, and you're getting us animals a bad name in the district by your furious driving and your smashes and your rows with the police. Independence is all very well, but we animals never allow our friends to make fools of themselves beyond a certain limit; and that limit you've reached.'[6]

Badger lectures Toad, illustration by Nancy Barnhart from a 1922 edition of *The Wind in the Willows*.

Badger stands in for respectable class sensibility and conventional behaviour, which he imposes on his unconventional friend. In his cosy bachelor's domain, the unruly is the sphere of the working-class hooligan weasels in the Wild Wood, a world to which, as landed gentry, Toad significantly does not – or at least *should not* – belong. (Modelled in part on the flamboyant and tradition-flaunting Oscar Wilde, the aristocratic Toad stands somewhat apart from the domesticating morality of these stolid, upper-middle-class mammals.[7]) Badger's 'down-at-heels bourgeois quietude' is the calm dignity of an idealized and privileged past; Toad's mechanical faddishness and the uppity actions of the Wild Wooders destabilize this world and its foundations, but stalwart Badger stands as the threshold guardian of nostalgia's domain.[8]

The sharply defined class hierarchy among the animals in Grahame's novel was taken up decades later by novelist Jan Needle in *Wild Wood* (1981), in which the events of *The Wind in the Willows* are retold through the working-class perspectives of the ferrets, weasels and stoats. These mustelids actively challenge the hereditary wealth and class bias of 'a rich and indolent gentleman by the name of Toad' who 'indulged his whims and fancies in a way that sometimes made a hard-working animal feel more than a little bitter'. The deprivations of the Wild Wood mark the territory of those labouring animals, while 'The River Bank was where the smart set lived'.[9] Informed by a very different cultural atmosphere regarding class relations, animal welfare and land conservation from that of 1908, the Badger of Needle's account is far from the crusty but benevolent patriarch of Grahame's story. Instead, in the words of Boddington Stoat, he's 'a traitor to his class. He's had to work, even if he's well-off now. He's letting us down. He's joined the other side.'[10] The qualities that make Badger a charmingly old-fashioned figure in *Willows* make him a reactionary bully in *Wild Wood*, as he is the forceful

Bob Hoskins as an endearingly gruff Badger in a television adaptation of Grahame's novel, 2006.

advocate of an inequitable status quo that arbitrarily deprives some animals and enriches others.

Actors and filmmakers have emphasized different aspects of Badger's personality in the numerous small- and large-screen treatments of *The Wind in the Willows*; some have created almost unrecognizable versions of the venerable patriarch and his friends. In *The Adventures of Ichabod and Mr Toad* (1949), one of the earliest and least successful translations to date, the Disney cartoon Badger is given a name – Angus MacBadger – and is the somewhat doddering stereotype of a penny-pinching Scotsman. Here Badger's primary role is to complain about Toad's financial feck-lessness. Mole, Ratty and Badger are all very much supporting characters – it is (J. Thaddeus) Toad who is the adventure hero of this short film. Other versions of varying success include vocal or live-action performances of Badger by such distinguished actors as José Ferrer, Michael Gambon, Nicol Williamson and, most recently, an endearingly gruff turn by Bob Hoskins, complete with striped black and white wig.

The most faithful and successful adaptations, however – and the only ones to fully articulate the melancholic longing at the heart of Grahame's tale – are the stop-motion puppetry films and television series by UK-based Cosgrove Hall Productions. In these beautifully rendered animated adventures, which aired on British and American television from 1983 to 1989 with lifelike animal puppets, Badger is portrayed with gravitas by the veteran thespian and voice actor Michael Hordern. These productions remain among the most ambitious and well-executed representations of a badger character in popular culture, staying true to both the spirit and tone of Grahame's classic tale.

### BRUTALIZED BADGERS

Of course, Mr Badger is neither the first nor the last literary badger. But until Grahame's book, at least as far back as the tenth century, the dominant visual and literary representations of Eurasian badgers were as targets of human violence. In an excerpt from the Old English poetry codex the Exeter Book, we find this riddle:

> My neck is white and my head is yellow,
> my sides the same. Swift I am on my feet,
> I bear a battleweapon. On my back hair stands,
> as on my cheeks. Two ears tower over
> my eyes. On pointed toes I step
> on the green grass. For me sorrow is decreed,
> if a fierce warrior finds
> me hidden where I, bold with my children,
> inhabit the dwelling; [if] I remain there
> with my young offspring when the stranger comes
> to my door, for them death is decreed . . .
> if I can lead my family,

dear and akin, by a secret way
through a hole in the hill, afterwards I need not
fear a bit the battle with the slaughterous dog.
If the foe should mount with malice,
seek me on the path, the encounter
on the narrow path will not fail him
after I reach the top of the hill
and strike the enemy with violence,
with javelins, the one whom I long fled.[11]

Some critics have argued that the creature described here is a fox or a hedgehog, but the Eurasian badger seems a close fit, too. The riddle might allude to the badger's rolling gait, as well as the 'battleweapon', the 'javelins' that are its thick digging claws, which make it a worthy opponent of its iconic canine aggressors. The badger is a courageous and formidable adversary, one who cunningly defends family in the open air, not in the vulnerable sett. Badgers and their persecutors are thus inextricably connected, even in what might be one of the earliest textual references. (We will focus on this relationship in more detail in chapter Four.)

In later medieval hunting texts, Eurasian badgers come to greater if inglorious prominence. They typically appear as just one of numerous prey species, particularly in the famed *Livre de la chasse* (*Book of the Hunt*, 1387–9). The book's author, the French nobleman Gaston Phoebus (Gaston III, Comte de Foix), clearly had little regard for either the sporting or food value of badgers. In Middle English texts badgers are also markedly beneath the dignified interest of a noble huntsman, as they are categorized as vermin rather than the more respectable venery or chase animals such as harts, boars and bears.[12] (Foxes were similarly disregarded until the eighteenth century, after relentless hunting exterminated or dramatically reduced populations of the more desirable wolves

coment on le doit chaſſier on
le prēt aux chies aux leuriers
aux laqs et es cordes aïſi co
me fait le loup mais nō pas
ſi fort

and bears.[13]) This attitude continues in Elizabethan and Jacobean drama: after having his sister executed for marrying a man beneath her station, the mad Duke Ferdinand in John Webster's bloody seventeenth-century tragedy *The Duchess of Malfi* intones, 'I'll go hunt the badger by owl-light:/'Tis a deed of darkness'. Ferdinand's desire to hunt at night reflects his wicked pettiness and corruption, not the elevated masculinity associated with hunting nobility in the daytime.[14]

Keith Thomas observes that 'it was between 1500 and 1800 that there occurred a whole cluster of changes in the way in which men and women, at all social levels, perceived and classified the natural world around them . . . The relationship of man to other species was redefined; and his right to exploit those species for his own advantage was sharply challenged.'[15] By the nineteenth century, badgers were no longer so broadly dismissed, derided or condemned, at least not among those influenced by Romanticism and its elevation of nature to a state of sublime grandeur. In a country increasingly transformed by industrialization and its associated social and environmental disruptions, badgers gradually came to represent the fragility of imperilled wild animals and rural places and peoples. In one of numerous relevant sonnets, John Clare, an English 'peasant poet' most famous for *The Shepherd's Calendar* of 1827, offers a powerful indictment of badger baiting by chronicling the creature's courageous determination:

The frighted women take the boys away,
The blackguard laughs and hurrys on the fray.
He trys to reach the woods, and awkward race,
But sticks and cudgels quickly stop the chace.
He turns agen and drives the noisey crowd
And beats the many dogs in noises loud.

Badgers from
*Livre de la chasse*
by Gaston Phoebus
de Foix, c. 1406–7.

113

He drives away and beats them every one
And then they loose them all and set them on.
He falls as dead and kicked by boys and men,
Then starts and grins and drives the crowd agen;
Till kicked and torn and beaten out he lies
And leaves his hold and cackles, groans, and dies.[16]

Written at a time of increased (but also highly class-focused) activism against animal cruelty and especially blood sports like badger-baiting, the badger sonnets reflect a cultural tension between Clare's conflicted self-representation: as an 'Unlettered Rustic' and brother to the natural world, and a poet of a more delicate, middle-class sensibility that he believed distinguished him from other rural people. The badger in each sonnet is shrewd and formidable, a worthy challenger to various human antagonists, including a woodman who tumbles into an unseen sett, a group of baiters who capture their prey on a midnight raid, and a tormenting pack of dogs. Sometimes the badger is a desperate captive fighting for its life, but in one sonnet it is 'tame as a hog . . . [and] follows like a dog' and 'licks the patting hand and trys to play/And never trys to bit or run away'.[17] Humans are at best a thoughtless force, at worst a torturing mob. In these complex and internally conflicted sonnets, the more sympathetic the speaker is to the badger and the natural world, the more negative the response to the working class that he blames for nature's diminishment.[18]

Following Clare, the Eurasian badgers of the post-Industrial Revolution tradition of nature writing in Britain deserve mention, given their explicit function as symbols of an imperilled land and, with it, a particular kind of Britishness that Clare's (and, later, Grahame's) work helped to popularize. These texts, which proliferated throughout the twentieth century, generally advocate passionately on behalf of an ever-diminishing wild world and often explicitly critique the ongoing practices associated with badger-baiting. Of the many in print, a few stand out as particularly engaging. While best known for his award-winning novel *Tarka the Otter* (1927), which inspired public outrage at the brutality of the otter hunt in Britain, the prolific writer Henry Williamson was also the author of *The Epic of Brock the Badger*, originally published in 1926, a harrowing and finely crafted account of the baiting of an old boar badger. Unfortunately, for all its unsentimental descriptive power, the deserving story is not among his better-known tales. More influential, perhaps, was the literary advocacy of the acerbic BBC television host, journalist and stalwart naturalist Phil Drabble, who was famously fond of the nocturnal creatures. His memoir of 1969, *Badgers at My Window*, offers a detailed and sympathetic though decidedly unsentimental chronicle of his experience of raising and living among badgers. It is a gentler and more amusing volume than its 1979 successor, *No Badgers in My Wood*, a fierce and often bleak critique of those who persecute badgers and other wild animals.

FANTASY BADGERS

While some badgers have been represented in a realist vein, the realm of the explicitly fantastic has proven particularly fertile ground for literary badgers. Lewis Carroll (Charles Lutwidge Dodgson) included some unusual badgers among his many odd and quirky characters. In *Through the Looking-glass, and What Alice Found There* (1871), the toves from the poem 'Jabberwocky' are described as being 'something like badgers – they're something like lizards – and they're something like cork-screws'.[19] Yet it is in his most ambitious and largely forgotten novels, *Sylvie and Bruno* (1889) and *Sylvie and Bruno Concluded* (1893), that more explicit representations of badgers appear, used to mock the social pretensions of the growing middle class. In the first book, the eponymous fairy children are subjected to trademark Carroll nonsense verse:

> There be three Badgers on a mossy stone,
>     Beside a dark and covered way:
> Each dreams himself a monarch on his throne,
>     And so they stay and stay –
> Though their old Father languishes alone,
>     They stay, and stay, and stay.

In subsequent stanzas the histrionic and bourgeois Father Badger and Mother Herring complain to one another about their children's lack of filial duty in remaining far from home; Mother Herring is particularly dismayed that her daughters spend all their time singing 'with a grating and uncertain sound' about what 'makes Life seem so sweet'. Eventually the younger badgers tire of the she-herrings' unappealing voices and return to their Father, but not alone:

> Gently the Badgers trotted to the shore –
>     The sandy shore that fringed the bay:
> Each in his mouth a living Herring bore –
>     Those aged ones waxed gay:
> Clear rang their voices through the ocean's roar,
>     'Hooray, hooray, hooray!'[20]

Unlike the title characters of Carroll's poem 'The Walrus and the Carpenter' in *Through the Looking-glass*, who similarly encounter disobedient aquatic youth – in their case, oysters – the badgers offer no harm to the herring, but instead bring them home to their grateful mother: the status quo has resumed, and the herring will no longer disturb their neighbours with inappropriate songs. Illustrator Harry Furniss provides whimsical pen and ink illustrations, and all the animals are quite lifelike save for their clothing and human accoutrements. Their animal otherness is subsumed into dull, respectable middle-class mores both in dress and deed.

Other literary badgers and their surrogates offer more spirit and imaginative scope, although it takes a bit of digging to uncover some of them. Given its romantic pastoralism and nostalgic re-envisioning of a rural England evacuated of French Norman presence, J.R.R. Tolkien's Middle-earth (initially explored by readers in *The Hobbit*, 1937) would seem to be the ideal setting for the indigenous badger. Surprisingly, given his nearly fetishistic enthusiasm for all things symbolically English, there are few direct references to badgers in Tolkien's work. The most substantive appear in 'The Adventures of Tom Bombadil' (1934), a mock epic

Badgers return the herring daughters to their mother in Lewis Carroll's *Sylvie and Bruno* (1889), with illustrations by Harry Furniss.

Van Arno, *The Badger Hunt*, 2005, oil on wood panel.

poem about an ageless woodland trickster who later appears briefly in *The Lord of the Rings*, and in which Tom is briefly captured by a group of badgers after he invades their sett. (In *The Fellowship of the Ring*, 1954, the hobbits Frodo, Sam, Merry and Pippin visit Bombadil and he shares with them 'an absurd story about badgers and their queer ways', a clear reference to the extra-textual poem.[21])

Yet, while Tolkien does not often invoke badgers explicitly, his hobbits can be compared to Eurasian badgers; certainly they seem more badger than rabbit, as argued by some scholars.[22] The Shire abounds with badgerish hints, gestures and references. Hobbits are innately social creatures and largely ease-loving, burrow-dwelling and amusingly gluttonous omnivores, yet also demonstrate fierce determination when threatened. The descriptions of hobbit holes and their interiors are not unlike those of badger dwellings (and, perhaps not coincidentally given Tolkien's documented praise for Grahame's novel, remarkably similar to that of Mr Badger).[23] Indeed, Bag End, the gentrified family home of Bilbo and Frodo Baggins, has more than a passing similarity to the deep, sprawling expanse of more established multigenerational setts, as does the massive collective dwelling of the Took clan, the Great Smials. The Old English *broc* is a meaningful surname for the Brockhouse family lines of hobbits in the Shire and Bree, and as the root for the Eastfarthing village of Brockenborings. Various hobbit family and place names make subterranean reference, such as the word for hobbits in the invented tongue of the Rohan horsemen (*kûd-dûkan*, or 'hole dweller') and the hobbits' own word for their underground dwelling, *smial*, which comes from the actual Anglo-Saxon *smygel*, for 'a burrow' or a 'place to crawl into'.[24] (This is also the source for the cave-dwelling Gollum's alter ego, Smeagol.) Other underground hobbit referents include the Tunnelly, Burrows (or Burrowes), Grubb, Smallburrow, Longhole and Underhill families, as well as the locales of Michel Delving, Little Delving and the Lockholes.

Tolkien's hobbits, for all their badger-like traits, are not the animals themselves, but other British fantasists represent the Eurasian badger more explicitly, though to different effects. Indeed, it is in the British fantasy tradition, especially for children and young adults, that some of the most evocative literary badgers make their appearance. Some of these stories, like Grahame's novel, are beast fables and animal fantasies (including Colin Dann's sentimental *Farthing Wood* series and its wise elder Badger), wherein the protagonists themselves are exclusively or primarily animals, while others are more general quest tales with animals as supporting characters. As we will see, some rare few literary badgers are cruel and vicious, but most are earthy exemplars of ideal virtues, representative of stabilizing tradition in a chaotic world, steadfast friends and eloquent mentors far from Clare's tormented badgers.

In T. H. White's *The Sword in the Stone* (1938), the first volume of his Arthurian saga, *The Once and Future King*, the humble servant Wart is taught a series of life lessons by his time-travelling tutor Merlyn in preparation for his eventual ascendancy to the throne of England as King Arthur. Wart learns about both the beauty and the horror of the other-than-human world through transformation into various animals. When he becomes a badger for his final lesson, he visits an elite older brock, who is writing a doctoral treatise explaining humanity's dominion over other animals. The badger sage observes that 'it is true that man has the Order of Dominion and is the mightiest of the animals – if you mean the most terrible one – but I have sometimes doubted lately whether he is the most blessed'. When Wart declares that 'Man is the king of the animals', the badger corrects him: 'Perhaps. Or ought one to say the tyrant?'[25] Wart remains enamoured of the romance of war, in spite of the learned badger's warnings.

In *The Book of Merlyn* (1977), the final volume of this highly political Arthurian saga, which remained unpublished at the time of White's death in 1964, Merlyn returns to the world-weary king on the night before Arthur's fated battle with the fascist usurper Mordred, and together they go to the badger's sett. In their conversation, the despairing king, the conservative magician, the leftist badger scholar and a few other animals debate the various virtues and vices of government and war, in the hope of convincing Arthur that the pending war is both foolish and avoidable.[26] Arthur's faith in humanity's potential for transformative change is renewed by these inter-species conversations, and although he still dies at the end of the novel, his death comes as a result of a tragic misunderstanding during peace negotiations, not from any lingering desire for war.

As in White's allegorical England, C. S. Lewis's Narnia (seven volumes, published between 1950 and 1956) is a world that abounds with humans and talking animals, though this medieval realm is decidedly concerned with the rights and proper sovereignty of the nobility. Whereas in White's tale many of the lesson-giving animals are among the humbler sort – badgers, ants, geese and fish – Lewis's series privileges the larger beasts of lore, most notably in the figure of the Christ-lion, Aslan. Narnia is a less coherent or internally consistent world than either White's mythic England or Tolkien's secondary world of Middle-earth; its creatures are a motley and disconcerting assemblage of creatures drawn from English folklore, Christian iconography, Greek and Roman mythology, and zoology from around the world.

Yet badgers abide here too, in the kindly character of the loyal badger healer, Trufflehunter, who aids the rightful king Caspian in his battle to return Narnia to its former marvellous glory against the mundane brutality of the usurper-king Miraz. Like so many of his literary kind, this badger is a bearer of hidden lore and long-buried tradition, which he shares with the treacherous dwarf Nikabrik, who wants to kill the injured young king:

> 'Don't you go talking about things you don't understand, Nikabrik', said Trufflehunter. 'You Dwarfs are as forgetful and changeable as the Humans themselves. I'm a beast, I am, and a Badger what's more. We don't change. We hold on. I say great good will come of it. This is the true King of Narnia we've got here: a true King, coming back to true Narnia. And we beasts remember, even if Dwarfs forget, that Narnia was never right except when a Son of Adam was king.'[27]

Like Grahame's Mr Badger, Trufflehunter represents continuity between the past and present, with the emphasis on the ongoing legacies of history. Loyal and true, and obedient to human nobility, Trufflehunter demonstrates his badgerish dependability through his dedication to Caspian. Though he is courageous, he is not the great hero. He is instead a companionable and even servile sidekick, one who makes possible the hero's great deeds through his (quite literally) down-to-earth character and unfailing loyalty.

Indeed, after the paternal Mr Badger of *The Wind in the Willows* and the many successive wise-badgers-of-the-woods clones, the most common character type is that of the loyal badger companion. This role may be at least symbolically connected to the cooperative biological relationships occasionally observed between real badgers and other species in their respective ranges, pairings that have taken on iconic significance of their own: the red fox in Europe, the coyote in North America and the honeyguide in Africa. In traditional tales in Europe and North America, that companion is often a crafty canine, generally a shape-shifting fox or a coyote. In these tales the solid Badger helps his mutable, mischievous friend gain access to desired food, weapons or lovers, but often ends up the target of canid trickery, as in the brief anecdote from Laguna Pueblo writer Leslie Marmon Silko:

> My old grandpa liked to tell those stories best. There is one about Badger and Coyote who went hunting and were gone all day, and when the sun was going down they found a house. There was a girl living there alone, and she had light hair and eyes and she told them that they could sleep with her. Coyote wanted to be with her all night so he sent Badger into a prairie-dog hole, telling him he thought he saw something in it. As soon as Badger crawled in, Coyote blocked up the entrance with rocks and hurried back to Yellow Woman.[28]

Here Badger shows little of the powerful medicine from the stories recounted in chapter Two, serving primarily as a trusting dupe to the more quick-witted Coyote. (In nature coyotes have been

Red fox protecting den from North American badger.

observed waiting behind a burrowing badger and quickly snatching prey flushed out by the badger's efforts.)

Given that red foxes and badgers similarly exemplify the wild places and time-honoured traditions of the rural world in European lore, and that they have been associated together as contrasting opposites in habitat, law, custom and persecution for centuries, their pairing in popular culture and literature comes as no surprise. One of the more fascinating stories of the fellowship between the crafty fox and the faithful badger is attributed to a sixth-century Irish saint, Ciaran (or Kiaran) of Saigir. In this account the animal-loving Ciaran found his initial Christian converts among the wild animals of the forest, including the symbolically significant boar, fox and badger. Of these, the fox alone slid back to his feral state of thievery and fled the monastery with Ciaran's sandals, returning to his former abode to eat them. Rather than pursue the fox himself, the holy man sent the dutiful badger to seek out the fox; doing so, the badger 'beseeched [the fox] to return to the monastery' (or, in one version, assaulted the fox and drove him back to their devout teacher), where the penitent thief was chastised for returning to his former ways and

124

abstained from food until Ciaran gave him leave to eat again. Thereafter, we are assured, the fox 'became pious like the rest of the animals ever after'.[29]

Later, though largely originating among the Dutch and then spreading through France, Germany and Italy, the medieval fables of the trickster fox Reynard became particularly popular in England beginning in the fifteenth century.[30] Included among many animal characters is the figure of Grimbert (or Grimbard) the badger hermit, variously Reynard's credulous nephew or cousin. When Reynard is brought before King Noble the lion on various charges, Grimbert is one of the only animals to speak on

Grimbert the Badger with Reynard and family, illustration by Wilhelm von Kaulbach, 1886.

Reynard's behalf. More conflicted is the folk tradition of the time, which held that foxes would defecate or otherwise defile a badger's home to drive the dignified creature out and thereby gain possession. Edmund Spenser would draw on this image in his 1591 poem 'The Ruines of Time', a partial lament for the death of Robert Dudley, the first Earl of Leicester, which figured the badger as the noble but fallen Dudley and the fox as the representative of his usurping inferiors. (W. B. Yeats later referenced Spenser's poem in 'The Municipal Gallery Revisited', 1937, but noted more defiantly that 'No fox can foul the lair the badger swept'.[31])

Attitudes toward both species changed with the times. The sometimes antagonistic, sometimes complementary pairing would continue in political caricatures of the eighteenth and nineteenth centuries, such as Thomas Rowlandson's scathing 'The Loves of the Fox and the Badger, or the Coalition Wedding' (1784),

Thomas Rowlandson, 'Loves of the Fox and Badger, or the Coalition Wedding', 1784, print.

THE LOVES OF THE FOX AND THE BADGER, or the COALITION WEDDING.

in which the eponymous enemies and political party proxies are joined together by mutual greed – wryly deemed 'Necessity' – and exploitation of the nation. Their wedding ceremony is presided over by the Devil, who dances with the couple throughout their self-serving marriage. (To one nineteenth-century commentator, Rowlandson's use of the badger is entirely appropriate for such critique, given that it was 'one of the most stupid, sleepy, fat creatures imaginable'.[32]) In the twentieth century, novelist and essayist Roald Dahl proposed a more benevolent fox and badger alliance, this one against menacing humans in his popular children's book *Fantastic Mr Fox* (1970), which became an animated film in 2009, with U.S. comedian Bill Murray as the unlikely voice of the Eurasian Clive Badger. The 1973 Disney film *Robin Hood* featured a red fox in the title role, and a Eurasian badger as the rotund but fiercely loyal Friar Tuck whose near execution (and subsequent rescue by the vulpine outlaw) is central to the film's climactic conclusion. Again in each tale the dependable badger is a secondary character to that of the shrewd fox, but his assistance is nevertheless essential for their mutual success.

This long literary history of badger loyalty and dedicated service is likely more familiar to today's readers through J. K. Rowling's seven-volume *Harry Potter* series (1997–2007) and their associated films. Hogwarts School of Witchcraft and Wizardry, located somewhere deep in the magical mists of Scotland, sorts its sorcerous students by four animal-themed houses, and selection to the chosen house is largely, though not exclusively, predicated on a student's character and moral orientation. Gryffindor's house arms are represented on the novels' frontispiece by a lion (with echoes of both Lewis's noble Aslan and the lion of Elizabeth II's Arms of Dominion). This elevated house is composed of children 'brave at heart/Their daring, nerve and chivalry/Set [the house] apart'. Students in the snake-house of Slytherin are 'cunning folk' who 'use any means/To achieve their ends', while those in Ravenclaw, represented by an eagle, are of 'a ready mind,/Where those of wit and learning,/Will always find their kind'. The final house – and the most modest in its ambitions and the least significant narrative presence in the books – is Hufflepuff. Represented by a stoutish Eurasian badger, it is the house where students 'are just and loyal,/Those patient Hufflepuffs are true/And unafraid of toil'.[33] (Interestingly, Rowling's initial choice for the Hufflepuff symbol was a bear, but she changed it to a badger prior to the first book's publication, thus making it the least regal and most idiosyncratic of all the house mascots.[34])

Hufflepuffs are the garden- and kitchen-wise, the sometimes slow but generally genial comic effect, the unexpectedly courageous, and the earthy, eager sidekicks and loyal supporting characters.[35] Hufflepuff is the most inclusive house, measuring generous spirit above academic rank, and its students show less of the reckless glory-seeking of students in other houses. Unlike the Gryffindor heroes Harry Potter, Hermione Granger and Ron Weasley, Hufflepuffs are generally in the background, with little of the romance, menace or high daring accorded to the more dramatic and iconic lion, snake and eagle. (Notable exceptions

The Hufflepuff house mascot from the original Hogwarts coat of arms in J. K. Rowling's *Harry Potter and the Philosopher's Stone* (1997).

include Hufflepuff's courageous Cedric Diggory, a popular Hogwarts student who is murdered after he and Harry win the Triwizard Cup, and the participants in the climactic Battle of Hogwarts, where the fiercely loyal Hufflepuffs are second only to House Gryffindor in their willingness to fight the murderous Lord Voldemort and his forces.) The domestic comforts of their life at the school evoke those of Bilbo Baggins's hobbit hole, or Mr Badger's subterranean dwelling in the Wild Wood: 'The Hufflepuff common room . . . is a very cosy and welcoming place, as dissimilar as possible from Snape's dungeon. Lots of yellow hangings, and fat armchairs, and little underground tunnels leading to the dormitories, all of which have perfectly round doors, like barrel tops.'[36] This is a comfortable and by now familiar badgerish burrow, a safe sett for Hufflepuff's human cete.

There are scores of other Eurasian badgers in children's fiction, but only a few extend beyond conventional depictions, and there are fewer still that reflect the behaviours of actual badgers. In the popular Rupert the Bear comic strips, book collections and animated series, Rupert's best friend Bill Badger would hardly be out of place in Hufflepuff house, as he embodies the virtues of loyalty and trustworthiness, though he is fully Rupert's social equal. Children's book writer Denys Watkins-Pitchford (who published under the name BB) wrote a series of nine popular novels between 1957 and 1969 about the adventures of the canal-boating Bill Badger and his friends; though largely unknown now, his work has a loyal fan base and even includes an international literary society dedicated to his corpus.[37] More prominent recent additions to the literature are the badgers who appear in the 22-volume *Redwall* book series (and short-lived animated cartoon) of medieval animal fantasies by Brian Jacques, published from 1986 until his death in 2011. Here badgers exemplify the warrior ethos discussed in chapter Two: they are 'fated creatures, with many facets to their nature. They are noble, wise, warlike, loving and vengeful, as their nature dictates them to be – feared and admired but above all, respected.'[38] Far from the domesticated understatement of the Hufflepuff sidekicks, the great Badger Lords and Ladies of the volcano fortress of Salamandastron are figures of powerful purpose in the novels, fearsome foes and wise leaders. Jacques's badgers perhaps drift too far toward the idealized and overwrought extreme, as their virtues are unimpeachable and their vices few, but they remain among the more distinctive Eurasian badgers on page or screen.

## THE LITERARY *TAXIDEA*

After the Eurasian badger it is the North American species that is most represented in children's books, poems, novels, television commercials, sitcoms, televised sport and film. Neither as internationally influential as its Eurasian counterparts nor among the most iconic North American beasts – the bald eagle in the u.s., the beaver and moose in Canada, and the golden eagle and snake of Mexico – this badger nevertheless has as rich a literary history as its more class-conscious European cousin.

Many Americans' first encounter with a badger would be either on televised football games featuring the antics of the University of Wisconsin's Bucky Badger mascot, or in children's books. For example, Laura Ingalls Wilder's *On the Banks of Plum Creek* (1937) includes a full chapter on young Laura's encounter with a menacing badger on her way to a forbidden swimming hole. Yet more prominent among these works is the little badger by the name of Frances. In a series of seven popular books by American expatriate Russell Hoban (with most illustrated by his former wife Lillian), the preschool-aged Frances explores her world and learns numerous social lessons, such as going to bed at proper times, not being finicky at meals, and learning to be a caring sister to her siblings Gloria and Albert. Dating from 1960 to 1972, the books are still in print thanks in large part to Hoban's wry prose and Frances's own endearing pluckiness, and reached a new generation of children worldwide in 2008 courtesy of digital animation by the Jim Henson Company. Hoban originally conceived of Frances as a human girl, but the illustrator of the first volume, Garth Williams, drew her as a

Frances the Badger hesitates to go to bed, from Russell Hoban's classic *Bedtime for Frances*, art by Garth Williams.

young badger, and that version remained in Lillian Hoban's subsequent art.[39] (Williams was the iconic illustrator of another classic animal tale for children: E. B. White's *Charlotte's Web*.)

For Indigenous and nature writers, the badger is more than just a symbol; it is also neighbour, kin or both, though even here it remains elusive. In Native literature, badgers surface on occasion, nearly always elusive in their narrative function, more often symbols than characters in their own right. Here, too, the traditional cultural and medical associations of badgers and bears continue. For example, in his Pulitzer Prize-winning novel *House Made of Dawn* (1968), Kiowa-Cherokee writer N. Scott Momaday tells the story of Abel, a young Pueblo veteran struggling to reintegrate into his community after the traumas of war and cultural dislocation. In the course of the novel, he has an affair with a white tourist, Angela St John, who associates him in her erotic imagination with both a badger and a bear – the former creature bleeds into the latter, and both are figured as elemental symbols of subterranean vitality and sensual power.[40]

The most expansive of these badger/bear stories actually precedes Momaday's brief reference by more than 60 years. Gertrude Simmons Bonnin (pen name Zitkála-Ša), who lived from 1876 to 1938, was a Dakota Sioux writer, performer and political activist who worked in many genres to present a more complex image of Native Americans than the noble and ignoble savages in vogue at the time.[41] Among her many works, which include poetry, fiction, essays and compositions for an opera, is the story 'The Badger and the Bear' (1901), based on a traditional Sioux tale about the origins of the culture hero Blood-clot Boy and adapted somewhat to emphasize contemporaraneous politics.

In the story, a family of badgers lives a self-sufficient life in a simple but comfortable home. One day a dishevelled black bear comes begging for food and the badgers welcome him to share their

Alan Syliboy (Mi'kmaq), *Badger Study #5*, 2008, acrylic on canvas.

meal. Every day father badger returns with food, and the bear returns to eat his fill of the best cuts of meat, becoming such a regular visitor that 'mother badger placed a fur rug in his place. She did not wish a guest in her dwelling to sit upon the bare hard ground.'[42]

Not satisfied with the kindness that has brought him to full health from the brink of starvation, the bear one day drives the badgers from their dwelling and lays claim to their possessions, including the father's arrows and their bags of meat. Without arrows, father badger is unable to provide for his hungry family, so he returns to beg for food, only to be cruelly rebuffed. On his second visit, however, the badger spots a clot of fresh bison blood, which he hides as he returns to his family's crude shelter. To purify himself and the blood clot, he builds a sweat lodge and enters with the clot, whereupon he begins to pray:

133

'Great Spirit, bless this little buffalo blood'. Then he arose, and with a quiet dignity stepped out of the lodge. Close behind him some one followed. The badger turned to look over his shoulder and to his great joy he beheld a Dakota brave in handsome buckskins. In his hand he carried a magic arrow. Across his back dangled a long fringed quiver. In answer to the badger's prayer, the avenger had sprung from out of the red globules.

'My son!' exclaimed the badger with extended right hand.

'How, father', replied the brave; 'I am your avenger!'[43]

When the badger explains that he again plans to beg the bear for meat to feed his suffering family, the blood-clot warrior says that he will join him: 'This made the old badger happy. He was proud of his son. He was delighted to be called "father" by the first human creature.'[44] Whatever their biological differences, the badgers and the newborn Dakota warrior are kin, and it is through mutual respectful participation in familial service that right balance is restored. They return to the great badger lodge, in which the bear and all his family have taken residence, for a final confrontation. One threatening look from the badger's blood-clot son sends the bears running in terror, and as the badgers reclaim their home, the young avenger departs to continue his marvellous travels across the world.

Published at the turn of the twentieth century, 'The Badger and the Bear' addresses issues that were of concern throughout Bonnin's career – namely, the numerous cultural, physical and spiritual devastations that accompanied the theft of Indigenous lands and resources by white settlers, and the base ingratitude at the heart of such actions. Traditional Sioux values of generosity and hospitality are the foundation of the badgers' behaviour, and their betrayal by the bear family reflects similar betrayals experienced by the Sioux peoples through increased American intrusions into their lands.

Non-Indigenous nature writers, too, have used badgers for aesthetic and pedagogical purpose. Canadian naturalist and co-founder of the Boy Scouts of America Ernest Thompson Seton gave extensive attention to badgers in a few of his natural histories and fictionalized animal tales, especially in 'Old Silver-grizzle – The Badger', from *Wild Animals at Home* (1913). While a careful observer of animal behaviour and a lifelong literary defender of wildlife and wild places, he was also inclined toward grand sentimentality in his many works. 'Old Silver-grizzle' is particularly excessive in this regard: Seton recounts the ostensibly factual tale of Harry, a lost Manitoba boy fed and cared for by a wounded she-badger. He is found by his human family after a few weeks and returns home, and the badger follows to become 'an established member of the family', even sleeping alongside the boy at night. Alas, their peaceable kingdom is short-lived, as the badger

Xhico, *Badger Boy Mitosis*, 2011.

is killed by the brutish 'halfbreed' trapper Grogan while sunning herself outside the door, and Harry is for a short time driven mad with grief, plaintively crying 'My Badgie! my Badgie!' in his delirium.[45] (Though the characters' names are different, Allan W. Eckert's award-winning young adult novel of 1971, *Incident at Hawk's Hill*, closely follows the narrative structure of Seton's unacknowledged account. In 1975 Disney adapted the novel for television as *The Boy Who Talked to Badgers*.)

Later tales by nature and rural writers are less emotionally manipulative, but they still tend toward emphasizing idealized human characteristics. In his 1990 children's book *Crow and Weasel*, Barry Lopez writes about two young beast-men, Crow and Weasel, who set off on a journey to learn of their own strengths and the proper relationship of their people to the rest of the cosmos, a pseudo-Plains Indian vision quest mingled with a somewhat over-determined environmental message.[46] On their journey Crow and Weasel encounter Badger, a subterranean storyteller, a gift-giver and teacher. She helps Weasel to discover his own storytelling skills by continually interrupting with questions, which Crow rightly identifies as her effort 'to help him, by teaching him to put the parts together in a good pattern, to speak with a pleasing rhythm, and to call on all the details of memory'.[47]

Far different creatures from Lopez's wise she-badger are to be found in 'The Old Badger Game' by Annie Proulx, perhaps best known for her short story 'Brokeback Mountain' (1997). This tale focuses on three 'old bachelor badgers' who live 'concerned with food, sunbathing, and property lines'.[48] The plot, such as it is, concerns one badger's thwarted romance with a rancher's wife: he is smitten, but she is simply interested in using his unique reddish coat as a fashion accessory. The rancher arrives with a gun and Red wisely abandons his courtship. This is no deep character study; rather, it is a light and playful tale, with the badgers serving simply as commentators on and unlikely participants in the strange domestic dramas of human beings.

Other badger species have far less representation than their North American or Eurasian kin, and when they are present, they tend toward the negative. Aside from a few folklore references, hog and ferret badgers are almost never mentioned. The honey badger makes occasional and rather minor appearances in literature, generally as menacing figures. Ratels are included among the animal-bodied goblins in Christina Rossetti's erotic/religious poem 'Goblin Market' of 1862 ('One like a ratel tumbled hurry skurry'), where the bestial goblins tempt young women with their 'orchard fruits . . . /Sweet to tongue, sound to eye', but turn feral and ferocious when their wares are refused[49]). Robert Ruark, a Hemingwayesque sportsman and adventure writer whose later work frequently drew on his numerous trips to Africa, used the symbol of the supposedly castrating ratel in his final novel, *The Honey Badger*, in part to represent what he saw as American women's emasculating proclivities.[50] And in the animated film *Kirikou and the Sorceress* (1998), set vaguely in West Africa, the tiny eponymous protagonist faces down a stinking subterranean creature that vaguely resembles a ratel.

Indeed, while most badger characters of page and screen are benevolent, or at least amusingly cantankerous, some of the most memorable are what Angela Cassidy succinctly calls the 'bad badger', a broad category that draws on a wide assortment of negative attitudes toward the living animals. Focused on representations of the Eurasian species, Cassidy notes in particular Beatrix Potter's Tommy Brock, in *The Tale of Mr Tod* (1912), as 'one of the few negative fictional portrayals of badgers'. He is 'a

deeply unpleasant character, who as well as being sly and predatory is smelly, dirty, uncouth, and carries a spade (much like
baiters and diggers)', and who, after deceiving the benign country
squire Mr Bouncer, kidnaps the older rabbit's grandchildren to
eat.[51] Most literary badgers are faithful and trustworthy members
of the earthy working or middle class, often embodiments of
romantically idealized rural values, but not so Tommy Brock:
he's a lazy, treacherous villain whose cruelty is motivated in part
by his boorish class resentment of the kindly, well-to-do rabbits.

Some 'bad badgers' are truly the stuff of nightmares, or at
least rely heavily on the stereotype of badger aggression. The
Eurasian 'lendri' of Richard Adams's *Watership Down* (1972) are
shadowy but menacing enemies of the novel's rabbit protagonists.
In the independent film *It's All Gone Pete Tong* (2004), the hal-
lucinogenic chronicle of a DJ whose life spirals out of control as
he slowly goes deaf, the protagonist Frankie Wilde feverishly

Beatrix Potter's Tommy Brock, from *The Tale of Mr Tod* (1912).

The nightmare 'coke badger' from *It's All Gone Pete Tong* (dir. Michael Dowse, 2004).

faces down his drug addiction, which is represented by a man (actually himself) dressed as a tutu-wearing, cocaine-encrusted badger. And then there are the menacing badgers with more wryly comic purpose. In episode 250 of *The Simpsons* (2000), a vicious North American badger lays claim to the dwelling of the family dog, Santa's Little Helper. Bart and Lisa seek guidance on luring the creature out by turning to the website WhatBadgersEat.com. (*The Simpsons* animators subsequently created a real version of this imaginary website.[52]) At the end of the episode, and after the hapless family patriarch Homer is nearly disembowelled by the four-legged squatter in a failed eviction, a horde of feral badgers descends on the town of Springfield to ravage its human inhabitants.

We return once again to mainstream fantasy literature to find perhaps the most unpleasant badger character, in the popular genre fantasy role-playing game Dungeons and Dragons (D&D).

Although most badgers throughout the game's accessories and novels are benign animal companions or misshapen monsters, there is also the murderous werebadger. In the gothic-themed world of Ravenloft, the general character type is developed in Azrael Dak, a gleefully sadistic dwarf who revels in his unique powers:

> Azrael's iron-shod boots struck sparks from the stones underfoot as he ran to meet the assault. He balled his thick-fingered hands into fists in front of his face. Then his arms went slack, trailing loosely to his sides like broken wings. Claws burst from his fingertips. His heavy-footed gait became more certain, swifter. Fur sprouted in unpleasant gray-and-black tufts from his face and bare arms. A scream that was equal parts ecstasy and anguish blasted from his lips. The dwarf's entire frame convulsed, the bones of his skull grinding into a new configuration – a terrible mixture of dwarf and giant badger.[53]

Dak cuts a bloody swath through two novels, a comic book and various gaming accessories, first as the enforcing henchman of the death knight, Lord Soth, and then later as Soth's successor as the tyrant of the ruinous realm of Sithicus.[54] Stories about were-creatures always represent our vexed relationship with our animal selves and the natural world: that Dak's own brutality is embodied in badger form reflects not only well-established stereotypes about aggressive carnivores in general and badgers in particular, but it also explicitly renders Dak's evil legible only through its embodiment in beastly form. He may be a bully, a torturer, and a murderer, but in the West, where humans stand anxiously atop the hierarchy of personhood and social value, he is particularly depraved not because of his antisocial crimes but because he so fully blurs the line between animal and human.

Azrael Dak transforms into a murderous werebadger.

As the dozens of famous and obscure characters on Wikipedia's collectively compiled 'List of Fictional Badgers' make clear, badgers, it seems, are everywhere, but only when you begin looking for them. They are to be found in various and sundry short stories, novels, games and poems, not to mention children's television shows (including the much-loved 1990s BBC children's series *Bodger and Badger*), animated cartoons, sitcoms, films and Internet skits. They are rare but memorable figures in comic books: American Mike Baron's series superhero The Badger is a mentally ill Vietnam War veteran from Wisconsin who uses martial arts and his ability to speak to animals in the fight against environmental despoilers and white supremacists, while Bryan Talbot's acclaimed graphic novel *Grandville* features an anthropomorphized Eurasian

badger, Detective Inspector LeBrock, as the protagonist in a fantastical, pseudo-nineteenth-century Franco-England. A recent comic book series features a honey badger as the small but intimidating superhero.

They inspire personal decoration: in the American West and Southwest, where badger populations are stable, their claws are not uncommonly included in jewellery. They appear in more formal and ceremonial art, in paintings, as sculptural pieces, as musical instruments. Zuni and other Pueblo artisans include badgers among the animal subjects of their distinctive stone fetishes, and Badger continues to be prominent in Hopi kachina traditions. They also feature in acoustic folk music, such as the High Desert Band's memorable 'Badger in the Outhouse', about a grandmother's campaign against the badger who has taken over her privy, the surreal rock-rap anthem against the cull 'Badger Swagger', by Artful Badger and Friends (and which features a voiceover cameo by David Attenborough), and the popular viral video 'Badger Badger Badger', with dancing badgers, mushrooms and snakes popping up in a stylized woodland with a repeating synthesized refrain of 'badgerbadgerbadgerbadger'. And of course we cannot forget Randall's online contribution, discussed in chapter Two, which has made 'honey badger don't care' part of the popular lexicon across the English-speaking world.

Badger fetish carved by New Mexico artist Arden Toledo (Ramah/Zuni).

Yet even in these varied and imaginative realms badgers remain firmly rooted in a familiar popular mythology that is often far removed indeed from the behaviours and experiences of actual badgers. The arts can certainly inspire us to have more empathetic and compassionate attitudes toward the wild world. Yet the more distanced we become from that world, through urbanization and industrialization, the more potential there is for its other-than-human inhabitants to become shallow symbols and for the flesh-and-blood beings to be forgotten or actively disregarded. The sad reality is that no matter how respected badgers have been in various cultures and across various times, or how evocative they might be to any number of writers and artists, the baseline attitude of many humans toward these reclusive creatures is still one of suspicion, commercial exploitation or active persecution. And the price that badgers pay for those attitudes is a steep one indeed.

# 4 Uses and Abuses: The Persecuted Badger

Baited by Dogs, the Badger dies.
A cruel sport it thus supplies.
The Skin is by the Furriers bought,
And thus for gain & pleasure sought.
W. Belch, c. 1820

For all their biological complexity and imaginative significance, badgers throughout the world have experienced one constant in their varied relationships with humans: where badgers and humans meet, badgers suffer. Sometimes this experience is an unintended consequence of human activity, such as habitat loss and the thousands of deaths due to vehicle traffic every year in Europe and North America.[1] Very often, however, badger suffering is intentionally inflicted, through vermin control measures, commercial hunting and trapping, blood sport, or simply random and often astonishing cruelty. Two honey badger examples illustrate this point. In his memoir of a journey to South Africa in 1797, Sir John Barrow noted that:

> no animal is perhaps more tenacious of life than the ratel. A dog with great difficulty can worry it to death; and it is a species of amusement for the farmers to run knives through different parts of the body, without being able, for a length of time, to deprive it of existence.[2]

In the 1960s another observer reported shooting and wounding a ratel. As the gun proved inadequate, the travellers chose a more novel form of execution: they parked a Jeep 'with the front

Guido von Maffei, *Dachshunds on a Badger*, 1882, oil on canvas.

145

Road casualty.

wheel on the animal's chest, and it died some minutes later, still biting and clawing at the tire'.[3]

All badger species are targets of persecution for profit, protection or amusement. To be 'badgered' is not, as commonly presumed, a statement about the behaviour of badgers; rather, those responsible for the badgering are human. Quite literally, to be badgered is to be immobilized, brutalized and overwhelmed by ferocious opponents (generally trained dogs) until mutilated and/or killed. The term has largely lost its historical specificity and switched the order of aggressor, but the bloody sport of badgering continues today.

Whereas the previous chapters have focused on the honoured significance of badgers in the human imagination, this chapter will explore the historical and contemporary shadow side of that relationship, giving context for the badgers' often imperilled state throughout the world.

The hunting of badgers for food, clothing, medicine and entertainment has a long recorded history, but they have generally been less desirable than other game animals. Badger bones have been found in archaeological excavations throughout their historical range, but not in significant numbers compared to other animals: for example, at one dig in the eastern Nile delta of lower Egypt only a handful of honey badger bones were identified among hundreds of remains dating back nearly 5,000 years.[4] By the seventeenth century, rendered badger fat and distilled blood were occasionally referenced in European medical ('physick' or 'chirurgical') texts as treatment for various ailments, from mundane joint aches and intestinal discomfort to kidney disease, leprosy, impotence and even the plague; mixed with wine and

*Badger and Dogs, 1818, engraving by J. Greig.*

vinegar, badger fat even served as a treatment for sciatica.[5] Distilled badger blood was said to be protection against poison.[6] To combat memory loss, sufferers were advised to tie a badger's left foot under one arm.[7] But even in these texts, badgers are a minor concern, and they remain uncommon in most folk medicine traditions today.

Historically, humans have eaten all badger species. Eurasian badger meat has been praised by some gastronomes, who claim that the meat of young badgers is particularly succulent and not unlike the fatty flavour of pork, while that of mature badgers is 'very greasy and with an extremely strong game flavour'.[8] An Austrian recipe for 'jugged badger' calls for boiling marinated chunks of badger meat with 'laurel leaf, peppercorns, salt, red wine, sour cream and stirring in some apple sauce'.[9] Smoked or cured like ham or bacon in the UK and Europe, one commentator noted that the 'most useful comparison was to mutton. The meat was dark, succulent and strong-tasting, but in no way like pork, having a particular smell to it.'[10] Due in part to their own culturally conditioned food prejudices as well as general unfamiliarity with the local species, European travellers in North America ate badgers 'either as a curiosity or as a necessity'.[11] Among North American Native peoples, on the other hand, badgers were more subjects of ceremony than sources of protein. Today, badger consumption is limited primarily to rural areas in eastern Europe and Russia, as well as central and southeast Asia; due to the decline in preferred quarry, the honey badger is increasingly a target of bushmeat hunters in Zambia and elsewhere in its range.[12]

In some places, cultural taboos and biological dangers accompany the eating of badgers. The idea is anathema to many in the UK, especially as the Eurasian badger has become increasingly synonymous with the pastoralist ideals of rural Britain: one simply does not eat the symbolic representative of one's homeland, especially if that representative is a musky, subterranean member of the weasel family. Take, for instance, the case of retired Cornish civil servant Arthur Boyt. His predilection for eating road kill

Badgers caged for food in China.

149

led to ostracism and threatening phone calls from disgusted neighbours, with his badger consumption the focus of particular scorn.[13] Beyond social stigma are issues of safety. Health risks in eating badger meat are similar to those associated with eating under-cooked pork, and consumption of badger meat (especially as 'shaslik', a kind of badger kebab) was linked to cases of trichinosis in Russia as recently as 2002, accounting for 31.5 per cent of wild-game related cases involving children over a four-year period.[14]

More controversial than hunting or scavenging is the use of badger bodies as commercial objects. In most parts of Europe badgers are protected by strict legislation. Trade in their pelts, claws and other body parts is heavily regulated, and hunting is generally limited to closed seasons or targets specific crop-raiding

Lady Gaga in a badger-skin coat by designer Hermès, Bulgaria, 2012.

150

Within the illustration:

Pygmalion

Lundi 28 Octobre

———

Fourrures

Nᵒ 1140. **Parure** opossum naturel.
*L'écharpe* . . . . . . **180** fr.
*Le manchon* . . . . . **170** fr.

Nᵒ 1141. **Écharpe** renard façon sitka.
*Prix* . . . . . . . . **200** fr.

LE BLAIREAU

badgers.[15] Throughout Asia, both Eurasian and hog badgers are hunted for their meat and their skins, and Eurasian badgers are raised for fur harvesting, though precise information about this particular industry is difficult to access. In the North American fur trade, where figures are more readily available, annual trapping numbers have remained relatively constant since the mid-nineteenth century. Between 1842 and 1905 the Hudson's Bay Company killed an average of 1,200 badgers each year in its Canadian prairie territories (where badger populations are currently in decline).[16] Today in those U.S. prairie states where the North American badger population is stable, annual trapping rates (generally for depredation or for sale to the fashion fur industry) run just slightly higher in each state.[17]

*Pygmalion* costume illustration featuring badgers and a badger stole, 1912.

151

Badger pelts do not have the same cachet among furriers and their customers as those of mink and ermine. In a fur auction held in Toronto in 2010, North American badger was among the least popular of marketed species, with fewer than half of the 3,829 pelts purchased. By contrast, 100 per cent of fox (red, grey, silver and white), squirrel, opossum and even skunk pelts sold.[18] Badger hair is stiffer and coarser than that of its more lucrative weasel-kin, and thus it tends to be used in clothing for trimming or speciality regalia rather than full garments.

The most culturally significant use of badger hair today is in the men's sporran, a leather pouch worn in formal Scots kilt dress that drapes across the crotch at the front of the kilt, considered by Desmond Morris to be a 'form of indirect genital display . . . covered with symbolic pubic hair'.[19] Though many kinds of skin and fur can be used for the full sporran or trimming,

While a raptor is the animal focus of François Louis Lanfant de Metz's *The Hawk* (c. 19th century), a Eurasian badger sporran features prominently in the boy's attire.

Portrait of George Gordon, 5th Duke of Gordon, wearing a badger sporran, by George Sanders, c. 1830–35.

including horsehair, seal and fox, Eurasian badger is particularly prized, especially in Scotland. Occasionally the skin of the entire head (or mask) is used for the purse flap, and this style has been traditionally restricted to officers and sergeants in some Highland regiments, thus in some way offering more symbolic protection

A men's badger-hair shaving brush.

to the genitals or highlighting the bearer's masculine prowess and thereby keeping with symbolic sexual associations of badgers.[20]

Given the legal protections afforded to Eurasian badgers in the UK and western Europe, and the general commercial inaccessibility of hog badgers and ratels, it is the more widely trapped North American badger and Eurasian species in Eastern Europe, Japan and China whose hair and full pelts are most likely to be used for commercial purposes. In particular, the Eurasian badger's hair has found a variety of uses, including high-end paintbrushes, car seat covers and, most notably, men's shaving brushes.

Wet shaving connoisseurs prize badger hair for its quality and comfort. Prices depend on the grade and quality of the bristle, as badger brushes are deemed to absorb more water and be more comfortable for applying lather than nylon or boar bristles. (Having tried both badger hair and synthetic brushes, I cannot testify to any particular difference.) The ethics and sourcing practices of brushes have come under scrutiny by animal protection groups. This in spite of the insistence by luxury shaving enthusiasts and shaving brush manufacturers and suppliers alike that the badger hair trade helps the Chinese economy and environment, where uncontrolled badgers 'would quickly be regarded as vermin and a pest to agriculture', and that the industry is in compliance with relevant legal protections.[21] The evidence is questionable for the latter assertion. In 2006 independent mitochondrial DNA testing on various brushes manufactured in the UK, the Netherlands, France, Spain and Italy revealed hair from both unprotected hog badgers and protected Eurasian badgers in use by brush manufacturers, indicating illegal trade.[22]

In recent years some shaving brush manufacturers have released well-received synthetic models onto the market, which are generally more durable, more hygienic, less expensive, and use less soap than even the premium badger brushes. Yet the arguments in favour of such commercial use of badger hair continue, and justifications expand beyond issues of legality to those of ethics: if badgers are indeed 'vermin', then producing high-end shaving brushes from their fur is less stigmatized and can even be presented as a laudable, even charitable act. For such arguments to be effective, the perceptual gap between protected species to disposable pest must first be bridged. And with badgers, that gap is often narrow.

## MELICIDE: BADGER AS VERMIN

Mary E. Fissell defines vermin as those creatures that humans perceive as 'icky, dirty, nasty, disease-bearing animals who are out of place, invaders of human territory'; most importantly, 'vermin are animals whom it is largely acceptable to kill'.[23] Vermin are animals whose behaviour sets them outside the norms that humans deem appropriate. When animals intrude on our projected boundaries of body and home, impinge upon our livelihoods and industries (eating crops, injuring or killing livestock, raiding food supplies) or violate our sense of 'natural' order, they enter the category of 'vermin', and are thereby sentenced to death for presumed crimes against human interests.

The vermin/criminal status of badgers became official in England in the Tudor Vermin Acts of 1532 and 1566; according to Angela Cassidy, this applied to 'those animals the Crown believed to interfere with human activity', resulting in 'a generous bounty of 12 old pence per head: a high price only shared by one other animal – the fox'.[24] (The acts pre-date the elevation of foxes to respectable hunting quarry.) Badgers are among the infamous and injurious beasts in *The Vermin-killer*, an anonymous eighteenth-century handbook on dispatching unwanted creatures around the home and garden. The various pest species are listed

Dead Eurasian badger and gun.

alphabetically, with badgers appearing second after 'Adders' and before 'Birds, of all Sorts, Earwigs, Caterpillars, Flies', and 22 other creeping, crawling, flying, biting beasts. 'Badgers', the author assures us, 'are pernicious Creatures, and destroy young Lambs, Pigs, and Poultry'. To kill them, readers are offered the following advice:

Some take them in a Steel Trap, or a Spring, as Foxes are taken.

Some make a Pit-Fall about five Foot deep, and four long, making it narrow at the Top and Bottom, and wider in the Middle; then cover it with some small sticks and Leaves so that he may fall in when he comes on it; sometimes a Fox is taken thus.

Others hunt the Badger to his hole in a Moonlight Night and dig him out.[25]

In spite of their 'pernicious' qualities, badgers can nevertheless be quite useful to the vermin-killer in exterminating another household menace: 'take the Blood of a Badger, smear a Trencher over with it, and it will gather all the Fleas to it, and kill them'.[26]

Whether with farmers in Europe and Asia, ranchers in North America or beekeepers throughout Africa, badgers have often been persecuted for both real and perceived damage to human livestock and livelihoods. The claims against badgers are generally exaggerated, but deeply rooted cultural prejudices against carnivores continue to influence practice and policy, with often devastating results.

Take, for instance, the case of honey badgers and beekeepers. The ratel's nickname is well earned: in Ethiopia, 99.2 per cent of participants in a beekeeping study reported that the honey badger was the primary predator threat to regional honeybees.[27] Ratels have been more fortunate in their interactions with Ethiopian apiarists than those in South Africa. In the former, traditional forms of deterrence (such as strategic placement of thorny plants) have been successfully implemented, whereas in the latter, where such practices are uncommon, 'half of all beekeepers interviewed . . . recently admitted to killing badgers despite their protected status'.[28]

Beekeeping is a major industry in South Africa, both for honey production and, more importantly, for fruit pollination. Honey badgers are just one danger to a fragile livelihood – vandalism, mite kill and urbanization have had significant impacts on bee survival. Although killing them does little to diminish hive destruction or its associated financial losses, the hunting, trapping and poisoning of ratels – as well as increasing threats from poachers – have resulted in 'considerable population declines across the interior of South Africa, and [they] possibly have vanished altogether from some portions of their former range'.[29]

Poachers at a honey badger den.

Currently listed as a 'species of least concern' by the International Union for Conservation of Nature, many local ratel populations are decreasing, and a change of status to 'near threatened' is likely in the near future.[30] While there has been some success from recent conservation efforts to develop non-lethal apiculture practices and encourage the purchase of 'badger-friendly' honey, numerous challenges remain, with human prejudice foremost among them.

North American badgers face less sustained pressure from persecution as vermin, but they are not exempt from the threat. A painting of 1908 by William Herbert Dunton captures the danger most commonly associated with the badger in ranching country. Variously titled *The Spill* or *The Badger Hole*, the Southwest desert scene shows a hapless cowboy and his horse falling hard to the earth after the horse steps in a badger burrow. The action of the scene is powerfully rendered: the surprised young cowboy has fallen face-first to the red earth, and his horse is in mid-flip on a trajectory to land on its rider, with crippling or fatal results likely for both.

As with the honey badger, the North American badger is perceived as a threat to human economic interests, yet its population has suffered somewhat less than its badger kin from this association. It is generally the farmer's friend and the rancher's enemy. This badger has been trapped, shot and poisoned not because of its chosen prey (which, being rodents, are hated enemies of the agricultural farmer), but rather because of exaggerated and rarely confirmed rancher concerns about livestock injuries. The 2012 downgrade of the North American badger in Canada from 'not at risk' to 'special concern' status is in part due to active persecution by landowners as well as collateral poisoning from the widespread use of strychnine and other indiscriminate rodenticides.[31] Yet direct and secondary killing is far less a factor in those areas of badger population decline than are habitat loss and traffic fatalities.[32] Indeed, as in Europe as a whole, it is motor vehicles that currently pose the greatest population threat to badgers in North America.[33]

BADGERS AND BOVINE TUBERCULOSIS

On 1 June 2013 three political groups gathered on the streets of London in simultaneous rallies. The right-wing British National Party and English Defence League organized one protest, while human rights and anti-fascist activists gathered in direct response to the nationalists. The final rally – much larger than the others – featured protesters against the Cameron government's pro-cull policies. These also clashed with the nationalists, and it was badgers and their partisans who had the most memorable headline of the day: 'Far-Right Extremists Chased Through London by Women Dressed as Badgers'.[34]

Of all badgers, it is the Eurasian species, especially in the UK, whose politicized status as vermin has received the most media attention – sometimes insightful, sometimes absurd – especially in regard to the controversy over their role in spreading *Mycobacterium bovis*, the source of bovine tuberculosis. Though only recently in the broader consciousness, bovine TB is in fact an ancient disease. It is transmissible between most mammals through inhalation, ingestion and any open wounds or passage of secretions. And it is devastating to afflicted animals and the industries that rely upon them. While in the early stage infection is often asymptomatic (and indeed many infected animals never

Anti-cull protesters in London, 2013.

develop full-blown TB), symptoms of later-stage infection are gruesome, including extreme emaciation, crippling coughing and constricted respiration, diarrhoea and burst lymph nodes.[35] The only fully effective control in domesticated populations is the testing, isolation and slaughter of the infected animals; while extreme, this policy has been largely successful in eliminating TB from many herds in industrialized countries. Wildlife, however, have proven more difficult and much more expensive to treat.

Those whose livelihoods are most imperilled by bovine TB have been understandably vigilant in their response, though not always to best effect. As is indicated by the disease's name, at least 80 per cent of transmission takes place between cattle themselves. Scientists now know that badgers are a small source of transmission, along with nearly three dozen other species, including house pets. The mechanism of infection is still uncertain, but it is likely from inhalation of the bacilli in shared pasturage. The fact that badgers are infected *by cattle* is often overlooked. Dairy industry and farming advocates have long called for widespread targeted or general culls of badger populations to reduce the TB risk to cattle. But while numerous smaller culls have occurred since 1975, with some localized success for short periods, the long-term results have largely failed to reduce TB transmission. Badger advocates draw attention to the increasing number of large, high-intensity dairy operations in the UK. Bovine TB is a particular danger to animals whose immune systems are already compromised by stressful, over-crowded and nutritionally deficient conditions. Indeed, rates of transmission fluctuate but are generally on the rise in the UK.[36]

In the meantime, it has become 'a politically fraught issue in Britain, pitching farmers against the equally passionate and vocal animal-protection lobby'.[37] With animal lives and human livelihoods at stake, emotions run high and the two sides are easy to caricature. The media have represented cull proponents as either stalwart independent farmers struggling to make a living in the face of government and social apathy, or as reactionary badger-haters who reject objective scientific fact in favour of ancient rural prejudice. On the other hand, cull opponents are seen as dedicated anti-cruelty advocates fighting on behalf of an unjustly persecuted species, or as arrogant urban animal-rights extremists imposing their pastoral romanticism onto rural areas with which they have little contact and even less personal stake.

Just as cull supporters and opponents have been narrowly defined in popular coverage, Angela Cassidy argues that badgers, too, have become stereotyped into two categories: 'good' and 'bad' badgers, though the qualities of each have changed over time. In an extensive survey of the badger cull controversy in the British media and its relationship to the broader history of badger representation, Cassidy explores these two divergent themes. The 'good' badgers are often individualized, like Kenneth Grahame's Mr Badger. Their personalized qualities include 'being mysterious/shy/averse to social contact; intelligent/wise; and a brave/strong fighter when attacked'; similarly, they are seen as having 'intimate and longstanding connections with the land, [being] a "native" species, therefore ancient, and symbolic of British national identity'.[38] 'Bad' badgers, on the other hand, are diseased and vicious predators that threaten lives and livelihoods; they 'are more often discussed in the plural, and in a depersonalised way . . . In turn, this forms part of a complex of characteristics depicting badgers as an undesirable underclass: violent, disruptive, criminal and far too numerous.'[39]

The situation for both humans and badgers is, of course, far more complicated. There are farmers who love badgers and urbanites who consider them pests. For some, the cull is the best alternative of uniformly bad options, while to others the badger controversy exemplifies a deeper cultural disregard for wildlife, as seen in other social and ideological divides in the UK, such as the foxhunt. Industry losses are framed by badger advocates as being primarily economic, and for the largest and most intensive farming operations this is no doubt the case. But for the ever-diminishing numbers of small-scale farmers whose own livelihoods are driven by the public demand for cheap dairy products, the situation is much more complicated. Hugh Warwick offers the following observation:

> Many farmers are held in near-slavery by supermarket chains that bind them into contracts in which milk is sold to the retailers at a price below the cost of production. Okay, there are some extremely wealthy dairy farmers out there, but they only exist at the expense of the smaller farmers, many of whom have been driven out of business by the impossibilities of making a living.[40]

Similarly, the cull is not the swift and merciful process some proponents assume: before the 2013 trial cull veterinarians

The cull controversy in an editorial cartoon by Andrew Birch for *The Observer*.

warned that, given their peculiar physiology and nocturnal habits, 'it is likely that many targeted badgers will not be killed outright; the natural behaviour of those that are injured will be to try to return to their underground setts where they will likely suffer a slow and very unpleasant death'.[41] These concerns were validated after trial culls in Gloucestershire and Somerset in 2013, when an assessment by independent experts revealed significant failures in the quick-kill death rate of the 'humane' killing protocol. And internal documents revealed that the agency responsible for the cull, the Department for Environment, Food and Rural Affairs (Defra), was uncertain about what 'humane' kills would entail throughout the process: one of the more shocking reports indicated that the humaneness of the cull would be assessed in part by the cries of dying badgers, which would somehow be measured to determine distress and pain levels.[42] Death by bovine TB is a long and painful experience; so, too, is dying over the course of hours or even days from a misplaced gunshot wound.

In the cull controversy, science and policy have often been at odds, even when ostensibly 'independent'. This goes well beyond the 2013 killing season. Consider the conflict over the final report of the Independent Scientific Group (ISG) on Cattle TB in 2007, which remains one of the most substantial scientific assessments of the badger-TB link to date. In 1998 the Labour government responded to the growing crisis by forming the ISG on Cattle TB, with the expectation that the expert panel would offer clarity on what was and remains a polarizing issue. Almost a decade later, in 2007 the ISG issued its final report, a nearly 300-page, detailed analysis of the accumulated scientific evidence by an internationally respected committee of biologists, epidemiologists, veterinarians and other scientists. The committee chair, John Bourne, stated in the report's introduction that 'while badgers are clearly a source of cattle TB, careful evaluation of our own and others' data indicates that badger culling can make no meaningful contribution to cattle TB control in Britain. Indeed, some policies under consideration are likely to make matters worse rather than better.'[43] The ISG's findings confirmed the fact that, while culling was sometimes successful in reducing TB infections in the areas where badgers were killed, it ultimately increased TB transmission, as infected badgers moved from affected areas into previously uninfected cattle populations (a process known as perturbation). Most importantly, the evidence confirmed that the primary source of new infections was other cattle, not badgers, and that earlier and better testing of cattle would offer more hope of containing and reducing TB infection than was possible even with the wholesale eradication of badgers.

Sir David King, then serving as Chief Scientific Adviser, responded to the ISG report by bringing together five more scientists, who met in person for a single day. Within a month King's panel drafted a response that dismissed the ISG findings and supported a badger cull, to the relief of the pro-cull National Farmers' Union.[44] After political, public and scientific condemnation of the haste and accuracy of King's report, Rural Affairs Secretary Hilary Benn reversed the policy and that cull was cancelled. But it would return. In March 2012 the Welsh government decided on a vaccination campaign, abandoning its pro-cull policy from just two years earlier. In 2012 the Cameron administration planned a massive cull of nearly 100,000 badgers (up to one-third of the UK population), but it was delayed due to weather, an unexpectedly high badger population in the targeted areas in Somerset and Gloucestershire, and soaring security and implementation costs; a Commons vote of 147 to 28 against the plan was a further setback to the government's plans. (The vote followed a public statement signed by 31 distinguished scientists from the UK and U.S. and an open letter from Humane Society

International/UK, both strongly opposing the government's position.) It continues to be a major controversy, with sharply polarized positions on both sides. In autumn 2013 the Cameron government moved forward the trial culls and the resulting controversy became front-page news in the UK, with opponents physically hampering hunts on the ground and eroding public support through boycotts of businesses associated with pro-cull farmers, direct political action against pro-cull politicians and public awareness campaigns. These culls were halted early in November 2013. When far fewer badgers were found and killed in the trial area than anticipated, Defra found their central claim of a widespread threat to be untenable. In the meantime, opposition has grown across the political spectrum alongside increasingly costly and embarrassing public relations missteps on the part of both government and industry. Surprisingly, the failures of the trial culls have not stopped the momentum for culling – they have only made the government less transparent about future actions, which, as of May 2014, include the possible reversal of the 1982 sett-gassing ban.

Millions of pounds have been invested in the development of alternatives over the last decade, including oral vaccines that could withstand badger stomach acid and be palatable to badgers but not to cattle.[45] The research is promising for oral and injectable options, and test trials offer hope that a viable, affordable and effectively administered vaccine will soon be widely available.[46] Cull supporters argue that investing in vaccine development is expensive, impractical, and likely ineffective, offering no short-term relief and only hypothetical long-term benefits. However, the trial culls have quite clearly been exorbitantly expensive and demonstrably ineffective, and there has been little improvement in TB rates – indeed, rates in both wild and domesticated animals are increasing. Still, Defra insists on culling as an essential strategy

Shared fates: badgers and otters as hunting quarry in a 19th-century German etching.

in combating bovine TB. Why? What is it about badgers in particular that makes so many people insist that melicide is the best possible response to the crisis? In a sharply polarized debate that too often figures badgers as *the* problem rather than one of many complicating factors to an already challenging situation, they are likely to remain at the centre of controversy in the UK for the foreseeable future.

### BAITING: BADGER AS BRUTALIZED PLAYTHING

The cull, while a danger to badger populations, is also a matter of public policy, and one that involves open discussion and debate. Another rising threat is far more clandestine. In the UK, where the foxhunt ban also continues to be a divisive issue, the history of blood sports is both long and grim:

> Badger-baiting, bear-baiting, bull-baiting, bull-running, dog-fighting, cock-fighting, and throwing at cocks are the best known, but there were many more obscure ones such as goose-riding, where a goose with a greased neck was hung up by its feet and horse riders tried to pull its head off as they galloped past, and sparrow-mumbling, where men tried either to remove the feathers or to bite the head off a live sparrow, using only their lips and teeth.[47]

Any animal, domestic or exotic, could find itself the target of human cruelty, from the abovementioned creatures to horses, donkeys, leopards and apes. Baiting was the most common form: a wild animal was chained or otherwise restrained and then set upon in continual attacks by trained dogs or other animals. The immediate purpose of the sport was (and remains) to see how long the captive beast could withstand the repeated assaults before death. Badger baiting, though historically found in continental Europe, now seems to be largely limited to the UK and Ireland. While not an institutionalized custom in North America, badgers are often subjected to isolated brutality, especially torment by trained dogs, as are honey badgers throughout Africa. (In the U.S. the practice is known by the rather more euphemistic 'terrier work', but is no less horrific, and includes not only badgers but raccoons, coyotes, foxes and other small carnivores deemed vermin.) Hog badgers are under particular threat from hunting dogs throughout Southeast Asia, especially in Laos and Vietnam, but not, it seems, for entertainment purposes.

Baiting is related to the arena slaughters of wild and exotic animals in the ancient world and their function as communal entertainments, as well as the medieval use of chained bears to train dogs to attack human intruders.[48] Historically, baiting and other blood sports were intensely social and communal events that included religious, political, ideological and even psychosexual dimensions. People of different classes and backgrounds came together in the safely shared experience of mortal conflict, where the blood being shed was not one's own. Baited animals and their canine tormentors were alternately admired, pitied and scorned, serving in some way as ego surrogates for the audience. So commonplace were these activities until the nineteenth century that they have come into everyday English, and few of us give a second thought to the bloody history of nouns like 'pit bull', 'bulldog' and 'cockpit', or verbs 'to bait' or 'to pit against' someone.[49]

Bulls and bears were the primary focus of baiting entertainments given the size and strength of the animals, but badger-baiting was also popular, and it was less expensive and easier to arrange in smaller venues, such as the back room of an inn or a stable. It was also the subject of numerous celebratory etchings and sketches in the nineteenth century, as well as photographs in the modern age. (Today it features in furtive digital videos exchanged on the Internet.) The artist and amateur naturalist Thomas Bewick offers a powerful account of badger baiting from 1800:

Few creatures defend themselves better, or bite with greater keenness, than the Badger. On that account it is frequently baited with Dogs trained for that purpose. This inhuman diversion is chiefly confined to the idle and the vicious, who take a cruel pleasure in seeing this harmless animal surrounded by its enemies, and defending itself from their attacks, which it does with astonishing agility and success. Its motions are so quick, that a Dog is frequently desperately

Obruitur saxis Taxus, laqueisque dolosis.    Vel canibus capitur, frualeisque ligonibus antris.

wounded in the first moment of assault, and obliged to fly. The thickness of the Badger's skin, and the length and coarseness of its hair, are an excellent defence against the bites of the Dogs: Its skin is so loose, as to resist the impressions of their teeth, and give the animal an opportunity of turning itself round, and wounding its adversaries in their tenderest parts. In this manner this singular creature is able to resist repeated attacks both of men and dogs, from all quarters; till, being overpowered with numbers, and enfeebled by many desperate wounds, it is at last obliged to submit.[50]

In addition to its evocative description of the badger's determined struggle, this passage is notable for its observation that it is not only the badger who is injured in this pastime: the attacking dogs, too, sustain terrible lacerations and mutilations, ranging from the minor to the incapacitating and even fatal. Yet as investments of time, money and ego, the dogs are sometimes treated for their injuries, whereas badgers are subjected to almost unimaginable cruelty:

The affair is not subject to the rules of a contest where the adversaries are equally matched . . . To give advantage to the dog, the badger is handicapped in the first instance by being secured by a chain or similar strong tether. Should this prove ineffectual in preventing the dogs from getting mauled by a particularly tough badger, then the leg, or legs, of the badger may be broken. Even worse cruelty may be practised; the lower jaw of the badger may also be shattered . . . or sawed off.[51]

This is not meant to be a true test of will or skill, whereby the badger can defend itself and live another day. Rather, it is the sadistic celebration of an animal's lingering terror and agonizing death – human bloodlust enacted through tormented and fear-maddened animal proxies. Before the baiting can occur, the badger has to be obtained. One of the most common methods is through 'digging' – the unearthing of an actively inhabited sett, sometimes by as many as twenty or thirty men with shovels. To 'draw' one or more badgers from the sett, dogs specially bred for the purpose (generally terriers) are sent in to harass and prevent the quarry from digging its way to safety.[52] Terriers – from the Latin root *terra*, earth – are often used in the menacing of burrowing animals considered by humans to be vermin, such as foxes (thus the fox terrier), rats and badgers. Similarly, the German hound-terrier hybrid, the Dachshund, is named quite literally for its skills as a 'badger-dog', with a long body and short legs perfectly suited for pursuing a badger into its tunnels. The more vulnerable cubs and pregnant and nursing females are often killed for quick 'sport' at the digging site, as they are most likely to go to ground at the ostensibly protective sett. Larger and more robust males, when caught, would likely be transported to a baiting pit to meet their own brutalized end.

The reasons for baiting are many, as are its symbolic meanings, but the projection of human emotions onto the badger are central. Anecdotal evidence indicates that it is a primarily (though not exclusively) male pastime.[53] Anxieties and assertions of masculinity are significant elements in the unfolding homosocial drama, for it is not only the baiting space but the gathering together of men that shapes the occasion's cultural context.[54] Yet not all men, nor all blood sports, were or are of equal social standing in enhancing masculine or military prowess. Paralleling the accelerated social stratification and urbanization that accompanied the Industrial Revolution, popular and artistic representations of blood sports have reflected the class prejudices of the age, in the eighteenth and nineteenth centuries as well as today. The foxhunt became a broadly legitimized cultural practice of the upper and upwardly-mobile middle classes, while elite reformers gradually targeted other blood sports 'on two moral fronts: first was the genuine outrage against cruelty to animals . . . and second was the concern with the effect that such pastimes would have on the moral character of the working classes'.[55] Such representations tended to minimize the participation of the wealthy and titled in the wider range of blood sports, while pathologizing the participation of the working class in the same.

Badgers were included among other animals in sweeping protection legislation in 1835 as part of a growing movement of animal welfare activism in the UK. Not unlike the political divisions associated with the cull, the campaign against badger baiting, while worthily rescuing untold numbers of animals from torment and death, has also long been embedded in a larger struggle about class identity, and the resonances of this conflict continue in the amplified rhetoric of both opponents and supporters of the various badger culls. Kathleen Kete argues that 'the transmission of bourgeois values was openly a goal of legislation prohibiting public violence to animals on the streets of urban Europe . . . The barbarian others . . . were defined in part by their brutality to beasts.'[56] These 'others' were the urban poor, immigrants, Roman Catholics and those not of the ruling establishment. While the middle and upper classes also participated in cruel entertainments, when economically marginalized communities practised blood sports, reformers condemned the acts as dangerous evidence of cultural and political degeneracy. Class prejudice has often been intertwined with a genuine concern for animal welfare, and just as animals could represent the best qualities of human nature, so too could they be mobilized as representatives of the worst. Unfortunately, even today this can result in more danger to the

Although blood sports are illegal in the UK, badgers continue to suffer at the hands of baiters and the jaws of their dogs.

animals under question, as they become an increasingly polarizing symbol for each side's social frustrations. Thus, the ideological or moral position becomes conflated with cultural values and even identity, and a critique of the one means an attack on the other. The animal then becomes targeted as a stand-in for one's ideological, economic, and/or social opponents.

This practice continues today. In sensationalized media accounts in the UK, baiting and digging is stereotypically associated with organized urban gangs, lower-class Others who 'treat the countryside as a "rural playscape" in which they enact their professional and personal business' with illicit moneymaking and gambling as prime motivators.[57] While not discounting the fact that much of the broader category of wildlife crime is financial in nature, the Royal Society for the Prevention of Cruelty to Animals (RSPCA) has identified a more complicated situation with badger persecution, which seems to be largely localized around former mining communities, close to wild areas that are more difficult to monitor and protect, but drawing participants from a wide range of backgrounds and regions. Attacks on badgers are now filmed and shared on the Internet. Connection is made through chat rooms and on social media, and some participants travel hundreds of miles for a baiting. According to an official at the RSPCA, the motivation is about family tradition and recreation rather than financial benefit.[58] A recent BBC report indicates a spike in prosecuted attacks on badgers from 2007 to 2011, which some have linked to the public discourse around the governmental and industry cull campaign over the same period.[59] And although the overall population of Eurasian badgers is strong, active persecution in many parts of Britain has resulted in significant local decline or near annihilation.

LOOKING FORWARD

In his 1909 book *Life-Histories of Northern Animals*, Ernest Thompson Seton makes the following observation about the North American badger:

> Thus, as in every case, the more we learn of the animal the more claim it has on our sympathy and interest. To the casual glance the wild animal is a fierce, elusive creature, occupied chiefly with eating and running away. It is only on getting gently nearer that we realize the other half of its life, the side which shows love for the mate, its young, and the pleasant society of its own kind.[60]

As we have seen, while works of the human imagination might make such understanding possible, more familiarity is not necessarily a guarantee of greater 'sympathy and interest'. Sometimes the clichéd adage of 'familiarity breeds contempt' holds true, especially when that familiarity is coupled with fear or self-interest.

However and wherever they appear, badgers are burdened with a range of contradictory and often problematic associations that have built up over the centuries, sometimes travelling between continents and across cultures. The complexity of human attitudes towards badgers is thus the source of both their widespread persecution and their increasing appreciation. We close by looking forward, examining the efforts of the badger people for whom these shy, oft-misunderstood creatures are more than mere symbols, but are instead meaningful co-inhabitants of an increasingly vulnerable wild world.

# Epilogue:
# Badger People, Badger Futures

The world of badgers is in some ways analogous with the
human world. It is made up of large numbers of individuals
grouped together in discrete social groups, each badger
having its own distinctive personality and temperament.
Like us their behaviour is greatly influenced by their needs
for homes and living space and being social creatures like
we are, they too have their problems of learning how
to live together . . . and with us.

Ernest Neal, *The Natural History of Badgers* (1986)

Phil Drabble emphatically declared that he suffered from 'acute
and incurable *melophilia* . . . a rare and delightful ailment from
which I am thankful that I can never be healed . . . The only symp-
tom is a deep affection for badgers.'[1] If such an ailment exists for
partisans of Eurasian badgers, then I, too, experience this condi-
tion, though more properly what might be its variant North
American strain: *taxideaphilia*. But in spite of the sincere regard
that individual humans might feel for badgers, even at their best
these attitudes and relationships remain complicated and challenging. They clearly mean many things to us, but what we mean
to them is less certain – though their general avoidance of human
contact would seem a good indication of our place in their world.
For all that the subterranean symbolism of these twilight travellers
might enliven the human imagination, when their world and
ours intersect, it is too often to their detriment.

Even those who appreciate badgers can be implicated in this
problematic relationship. A few years back I was invited to speak
at the University of Colorado at Boulder in early November, and
added a few days to the end of my trip and drove three hours to

visit my parents in my hometown, about 10,000 feet in the Rockies. I left Boulder later than anticipated, so it was well past dark when I started across the last high mountain meadows before reaching home.[2] As I drove along the moon-bright asphalt and scanned the road for icy patches, I saw an odd shape huddled in the ditch on the other side of the rural highway. When I suddenly realized what I had seen, I slammed on the brakes and slowly backed the rental car to the spot where a massive male badger lay dead at the side of the road.

This was the Lazy-S Ranch, a family friend's property where I had searched for badgers as a child and never saw one; this was the open country where a family acquaintance had shot and killed a badger just a few months earlier, for no other reason than to see if he could hit it. After my dad angrily recounted that story, we'd discussed whether that had been the only badger on the ranch, thinking it likely given the relative scarcity of badgers in the area. It had seemed then that something rare and wonderful had been senselessly, irretrievably lost.[3] And yet here, right in front of me, was another badger.

My first response was to see if the massive male was truly dead or just grievously injured. There were no other cars on the road, so I stepped out and walked over. The badger lay motionless, so I tentatively reached down to feel his fur and then the skin beneath. No response, but the body was still warm – he had been killed by one of the few vehicles that had previously passed me on the road.

I am ashamed to say that my next response was fierce possessiveness. Aside from preserved pelts, I had never felt a badger's coarse fur in person; I had never until that point smelled the notorious musk (which was every bit as eye-watering as I had read). Aside from skins, skulls, claws and other bodily remnants on sale in shops around the region, I had never been so close to the creature with which I had such a lifelong, if entirely symbolic,

*The Badger*, from *The New Natural History* by John Arthur Thompson, art by Warwick Reynolds, colour lithograph (1926).

affinity. At the time it seemed more than coincidence that I should pass by at that very moment, where, I convinced myself, I could rescue the body from being mangled by subsequent road traffic. That night I took the badger to my parents' home with the intention of visiting a local taxidermist the following day. After a restless sleep, however, the whole event seemed both ghoulish and sad, so that morning Dad and I drove to a secluded aspen grove outside town and left the badger's intact body to the elements.

I did not kill the badger, but the truth is that in death he became a *thing* to me, an exotic object to claim, a pelt and claws and bones, not the vibrant animal he had been mere minutes before his death and my arrival. It was not until later that I pondered why he had been out in the bitterly cold November night rather than safe in winter torpor. Had he fed too little in the fall? Possible, as there had been a long drought that year, and prairie dog populations were low. Had his torpor been delayed or disrupted? Had he settled in at all? Was he perhaps seeking the potential mate lost to a single summer bullet? Again, I wondered if this was the last badger on the ranch. My dad has seen no fresh sign of badgers in the meadows since and is unlikely to see any in the future, as the local mining company recently purchased the ranch with plans to extend their earth-scarring open pit operation.

In this case, as in so many others, the badgers on the Lazy-S Ranch had found death when their world met with that of humans. And for all my sincere and well-intended interest in badgers and badger lore, my response at that moment was one more of laying claim to a scarce resource than honouring the life and senseless death of a fellow being. My subsequent encounters with living badgers have, I hope, been far more respectful, but this incident is a humbling reminder of how easy it is to shift to *thing*-thinking when engaging with other animal people from whom we are so often estranged.

The first major ban on badger-baiting in the UK was passed in 1835, but it was not until the more extensive Badger Act 1973 became law that harassment, killing or digging of badgers without permission from conservation authorities was prohibited. This was a good start, but difficult to enforce, so the act was amended many times until 1992, when the various laws were repealed and a comprehensive law put into place as the Protection of Badgers Act.[4] Further protections followed under the still-controversial Hunting Act 2004, which banned the foxhunt. Yet in spite of the increased legal protection, badgers in the UK and elsewhere continue to be the targets of various forms of intentional violence based on prejudice, fear, economic motives and simple cruelty. As Timothy Roper suggests, the problem is not the presence of legislation but its enforcement: badger protection continues to depend 'mainly on the vigilance and courage of ordinary badger lovers, and on the willingness of bodies such as the Badger Trust and the RSPCA to pursue offenders through the courts'.[5]

Dr David Badger and a small selection of his extensive badger collection.

While the RSPCA has the longer history and the long benefit of royal patronage, it is the grassroots Badger Trust that has become the most visible group advocating on behalf of badgers, especially in the ongoing debate on badger culling to halt bovine TB. Local badger groups have been a staple of conservation, research and activism in the UK for decades. In 1986 nineteen groups allied as the National Federation of Badger Groups, becoming the Badger Trust in 2005. According to their website, the organization has significantly expanded to 'represent and

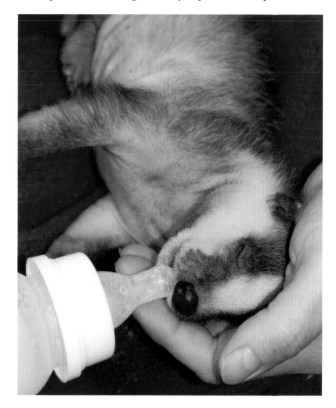

Nursing an orphaned Eurasian badger.

support around 60 local voluntary badger groups and around 1,000 individual supporters'. It also 'provides expert advice on all badger issues and works closely with Government, the police and other conservation and welfare organizations'.[6] (The recent anti-persecution 'Operation Meles' is an example of this effective cooperation.) The Trust is a national association but has affiliated groups in the Netherlands and Ireland; it has an international voice on badger-related issues, but its local work continues through rehabilitation of injured and orphaned badgers, observation of setts and reporting of vandalism and abuse, and education campaigns. Its regional groups are particularly effective in attending to the particular circumstances of local badger populations.

Honey badger-safe products logo.

The Badger Trust and other groups demonstrate through their various charitable, educational, legal and scientific efforts just how effective badger advocates can be in pursuing their goals of badger protection and public awareness. It takes nothing away from their success to note that their efforts, especially in the UK and Ireland, are also greatly assisted by the symbolic prominence of badgers.

This is not the case in other regions. In spite of the worldwide popularity of Randall's honey badger video, ratels continue to be seen as pests and threats to apiaries and farmers throughout their range, and as a result their populations are in decline. There is hope that recent collaborations in South Africa between ratel supporters and beekeepers in developing a 'badger-friendly' honey initiative will raise public awareness of the animal's threatened status.[7] Like the campaign for dolphin-safe tuna, economic incentives may be the best approach to convince beekeepers to implement practices that benefit animal and human interests alike. Although little is known about their conservation status, hog badger populations seem to be shrinking, and even ferret badgers are listed as vulnerable or near threatened by the International Union for

Conservation of Nature, with little if any organized activism on their behalf.[8]

Although North American badger advocates are less prominent and organized than their British counterparts, there are current efforts to stabilize some of the most vulnerable populations, particularly in Canada. The Nature Conservancy of Canada has a long history of working for badger population recovery, in large part through protection of vulnerable habitat and landowner education. In British Columbia researchers have worked since at least 2001 to develop a recovery strategy for the endangered subspecies *T. taxus jeffersonii*; in 2012 the population of the province was estimated at fewer than 410.[9] Similarly, on the other side of the country, the Ontario American Badger Recovery Team has been developing a strategy to ensure that the province's similarly endangered subspecies *T. t. jacksoni* achieves 'reproductively sustainable and secure populations . . . throughout its current range in southern and northwestern Ontario over the next 20 years'. In 2010 the Ontario population was estimated at fewer than 200, and these numbers were confirmed two years later.[10] Various u.s. states have enacted protections for resident badger populations, but there is little coordination between jurisdictions, and the protections vary according to population status, environmental and biological conditions, economic impacts and regional cultures of conservation.

BADGER FUTURES

'We just cannot leave the badger alone', Patrick Barkham remarks in the concluding pages of *Badgerlands*: 'We are compelled to find it, watch it, feed it, photograph it, poke it, catch it, torture it, defend it, kill it. Perhaps it is too big a mammal and plays too significant role in our landscape for us to ever leave it in peace.'[11] Considering how many thousands of years badgers have lived

A curious Eurasian badger examines a human visitor.

alongside *Homo sapiens* and inhabited our imaginations, it is hard for many of us to conceive of a world where they do not exist, or where their existence is so imperilled as to be almost extinguished. No matter how evocative they may be as symbols and images, they are, above all, complex living beings with as fascinating and impressive a biological history and ecological niche as our own, and that alone is deserving of respectful consideration. Yet badgers, like so many animals, face an uncertain future as a result of human ignorance, malice, self-interest or disregard. Even in places where they are currently protected by law and custom, there are daily badger casualties from baiting, shooting, digging, snaring, gassing and poisoning, as well as vehicle fatalities and displacements due to reduced or despoiled habitat. The effects of climate change, too, will no doubt add further pressure to what are already precarious conditions for many badger populations. They are determined and adaptive, but they are not invulnerable.

'There is still much to be discovered about many of the badger species', writes Ernest Neal, who until his death in 1998 was perhaps the UK's foremost badger authority, in his classic *The Natural History of Badgers*. He continues:

> Badgers have been a very successful group, exploiting a great variety of habitats on four continents. So far they have held their own with tenacity and have adapted to changes forced upon them by human activities. They have survived man's persecution for many centuries. Today they need our tolerance and understanding if they are to survive along with us.[12]

These are words worth heeding. Badgers are an ancient people, older in the forms they possess than we are. They speak to the dark mysteries of our own evolutionary past, and inhabit strange and secret worlds that we may know only through poetry, song and dream. They have survived momentous transformations of continents, climates and ecosystems throughout Earth's inhabited history. Yet it remains to be seen whether they will survive us. If they do so, it will be in large part because of the work of these badger people and others for whom a world without badgers would be a much diminished place.

Badgers have managed to endure, like so many other creatures with whom we share the biosphere, in spite of the ongoing ecological assaults of our particular simian selfishness. But the challenges they face are real, and growing. As Neal reminds us:

'It is their world too.'[13] May we have wisdom, humility and courage enough to honour our shared kinship as more than mere words, but as true understanding that transforms our lived relationships – for them, for us, and for the rest of the other-than-human world.

# Timeline of the Badger

| 23 MILLION BCE | 21 MILLION BCE | 10,000 BCE |
|---|---|---|

Marten-like creatures begin to descend from trees to become the earliest ancestors of badgers

*Taxidea* branches off from other mustelids and begins its gradual dispersion throughout North America from Eurasia

*Meles meles* (Eurasian badgers) return to Britain after the land is exposed by retreating glacial ice

| 1835 | 1908 | 1948 |
|---|---|---|

Badger-baiting is made illegal in Britain

Kenneth Grahame's *The Wind in the Willows* introduces one of the most beloved literary *Meles* to date: stalwart Mr Badger, friend of Toad, Mole and Rat, and enemy of his fellow mustelids in the Wild Wood

Ernest Neal publishes his first badger monograph, *The Badger*, beginning a remarkable 40-year career as one of the pre-eminent badger authorities and advocates in the UK

| 1992 | 1998 | 2007 |
|---|---|---|

The various legislative protections for badgers in the UK are brought together in the Protection of Badgers Act

The Independent Scientific Group on Cattle TB is formed by the British Labour government to study the links between badgers and bovine tuberculosis; their report is released in 2007 to considerable controversy

British troops serving in Basra, Iraq, are accused of releasing monster badgers on the local population, but the creatures turn out to be honey badgers displaced by habitat loss

| c. 1500 | c. 1700 | c. 1790 | c. 1830 |
|---|---|---|---|
| Renaissance painter Sodoma includes badgers in his fresco cycle on the life of St Benedict; Pueblo Indians include detailed badgers among ceremonial rock paintings in the American southwest | Jesuit priest Louis Jordan may be the first European to draw a North American badger in his *Codex Canadensis* | A hog badger is exhibited to audiences in the Tower of London's Royal Menagerie | John Clare pens his famous sonnets criticizing badger-baiting, which are published after his death in 1864 |

| 1949 | 1973 | 1986 |
|---|---|---|
| Buckingham (Bucky) Badger becomes the official mascot of the University of Wisconsin | The Badger Act expands protections for badgers in the UK | Nineteen local badger conservation groups in the UK join as the National Federation of Badger Groups. In 2005, with almost 60 affiliated organizations, the NFBG becomes the Badger Trust |

| 2011 | 2012 | 2013 |
|---|---|---|
| The ratel becomes known to online audiences worldwide through a viral YouTube video, 'The Crazy Nastyass Honey Badger' | A planned cull by David Cameron's coalition government is postponed; a majority of MPs vote to end the cull | Localized pilot culls begin in Somerset and Gloucestershire; badger advocates take to the country in direct action against the cull |

# References

1 NATURAL HISTORIES OF THE BADGER

1 John Ayto, *Word Origins: The Hidden Histories of English Words from A to Z* (Huntingdon, 2005), p. 46. Ayto makes the case that the word's early form, *bageard*, 'suggests that it may have been formed with the suffix -ard, as in *dullard* and *sluggard*' (p. 46).

2 'badger, *n.2*', 'badge, *n*', 'bauson, *n*', *Oxford English Dictionary Online*, www.oed.com; 'bêcheur, euse n.', 'blaireau n. m.', *Le Grand Robert de la langue française version électronique*, http://gr.bvdep.com. A current regional French term, *taisson*, can be confidently traced to the mid-thirteenth century (with its Latin source, *taxo*, even older), while another English term, *bauson*, referring to the blaze of white on the badger's forehead, dates to approximately 1375.

3 Caspar Henderson, *The Book of Barely Imagined Beings: A 21st Century Bestiary* (London, 2012), p. 173.

4 Quoted in Luc Brisson, *Sexual Ambivalence: Androgyny and Hermaphroditism in Graeco-Roman Antiquity*, trans. Janet Lloyd (Berkeley, CA, 2002), p. 137.

5 Pliny the Elder, *Pliny's Natural History*, trans. Philemon Holland (London, 1847–8), I, p. 68.

6 Giraldus Cambrensis, *The Historical Works of Giraldus Cambrensis*, ed. Thomas Wright (London, 1894), p. 44.

7 Richard Blome, *The gentlemans recreation in two parts* (London, 1686), p. 89.

8 Ibid., p. 90.

9 Baron (Georges) Cuvier, *The Animal Kingdom, Arranged According to*

*its Organization, Serving as a Foundation for the Natural History of Animals, and an Introduction to Comparative Anatomy*, I (London, 1834).

10  Thomas Bewick, *A General History of Quadrupeds*, 4th edn (Newcastle upon Tyne, 1800), p. 281.

11  Thomas Bell, *A History of British Quadrupeds, Including the Cetacea*, 2nd edn (London, 1874), pp. 158–9.

12  Kristofer M. Helgen, Norman T.-L. Lim and Lauren E. Helgen, 'The Hog-badger is Not an Edentate: Systematics and Evolution of the Genus Arctonyx (Mammalia: Mustelidae)', *Zoological Journal of the Linnaean Society*, CLVIII (2008), p. 375. The authors mistakenly refer here to *Helictinae* (a type of stinging fly) instead of the still uncommon but more accurate *Helictidinae*.

13  Charles A. Long and Carl Arthur Killingley, *The Badgers of the World* (Springfield, IL, 1983), p. 82.

14  Klaus-Peter Koepfli, Kerry A. Deere, Graham J. Slater, Colleen Begg, Keith Begg, Lon Grassman, Mauro Lucherini, Geraldine Veron and Robert K. Wayne, 'Multigene Phylogeny of the Mustelidae: Resolving Relationships, Tempo and Biogeographic History of a Mammalian Adaptive Radiation', *BMC Biology*, VI/1 (2008), pp. 10–22.

15  The Paleobiology Database (http://fossilworks.org) lists the maximum ages of identified fossils as follows: *Taxidea*, 10.3 million years; *Meles*, 3.2 million; *Arctonyx*, 2.588 million; *Mellivora*, 5.332 million.

16  Pamela R. Owen, 'Description of a New Late Miocene American Badger (Taxidiinae) Utilizing High-resolution X-ray Computed Tomography', *Palaeontology*, XLIX/5 (2006), p. 1000.

17  Koepfli et al., 'Multigene Phylogeny', pp. 7–8.

18  Jana M. Vanderhaar and Yeen Ten Hwang, '*Mellivora capensis*', *Mammalian Species*, 721 (30 July 2003), p. 3.

19  Huw I. Griffiths, Preface, *Mustelids in a Modern World: Management and Conservation Aspects of Small Carnivore: Human Interactions* (Leiden, 2000), p. vii.

20  John Knight, 'Introduction', *Natural Enemies: People–Wildlife*

    *Conflicts in Anthropological Perspective*, ed. Knight (London, 2000), p. 17.

21 Timothy J. Roper, *Badger* (London, 2010), p. 192. Male North American badgers also have abdominal glands; see Charles A. Long, 'Taxonomic Revision of the North American Badger, *Taxidea taxus*', *Journal of Mammalogy*, LIII/4 (November 1972), p. 729.

22 Gus Mills and Lex Hes, *The Complete Book of Southern African Mammals* (Cape Town, 1997), p. 202.

23 Long and Killingley, *Badgers of the World*; Ernest Neal and Chris Cheeseman, *Badgers* (London, 1996), p. 141.

24 Joshua T. Katz, 'How the Mole and Mongoose Got their Names: Sanskrit *Akhú-* and *Nakulá-*', *Journal of the American Oriental Society*, CXXII/2 (April–June 2002), pp. 297–8.

25 Neal and Cheeseman, *Badgers*, pp. 16–17.

26 Long and Killingley, *Badgers of the World*, p. 31.

27 In the most recent major badger monograph, the researcher Timothy J. Roper includes ferret badgers in the badger family but not the stink badgers or ratels.

28 As Koepfli et al. note, 'morphological similarity does not necessarily imply phylogenetic affinity' ('Multigene Phylogeny', p. 2).

29 'Badger, n'. 1c., d., and e. *Oxford English Dictionary Online*, http://dictionary.oed.com.

30 Antoine Le Grand, *An entire body of philosophy according to principles of the famous Renate Des Cartes* (London, 1694), p. 190.

31 William Sayers, 'Names for the Badger in Multilingual Medieval Britain', *ANQ*, XXII/4 (2009), p. 4. Sayers hypothesizes that the greyhound may have originally been named for its use as a badger-hunting dog based on this etymology, with the colour association a later development.

32 See Long and Killingley, *Badgers of the World*, pp. 179–202, and Neal and Cheeseman, *Badgers*, p. 71.

33 Joannes Jonstonus (John Johnston), *A Description of the Nature of Four-Footed Beasts, With their Figures Engraved in Brass*, trans. J. P. (London, 1678), p. 79; available at http://digital.library.wisc.edu (accessed 12 November 2013).

34 Comte de Buffon, *Natural History: General and Particular*, trans. William Smellie (London, 1781); available at http://faculty.njcu.edu (accessed 12 November 2013).

35 See Emmanuel Do Linh San, 'Utilisation des terriers par le blaireau (*Meles meles*) et le renard (*Vulpes vulpes*) dans la Broye vaudoise et fribourgeoise', *Bulletin de la Société Fribourgeoise des Sciences Naturelles*, XCI (2002), pp. 101–24.

36 Neal and Cheeseman, *Badgers*, p. 43.

37 Roper, *Badger*, pp. ix, 115–46.

38 See Niall Moore, Anne Whiterow, Paul Kelly, David Garthwaite, Julie Bishop, Steve Langton and Chris Cheeseman, 'Survey of Badger *Meles meles* Damage to Agriculture in England and Wales', *Journal of Applied Ecology*, XXXVI (1999), pp. 974–88, and R. G. Symes, 'Badger Damage: Fact or Fiction', *Mammals as Pests* (London, 1989), pp. 196–206.

39 Hugh Warwick, *The Beauty in the Beast: Britain's Favourite Creatures and the People Who Love Them* (London, 2012).

40 'Badger's Bloodcurdling Mating Cries Cause Helicopter Man-hunt in Germany', *Daily Telegraph*, 5 August 2008, available at www.telegraph.co.uk (accessed 12 November 2013).

41 Rudolf Altervogt et al., eds, 'The Mustelids', *Grzimek's Animal Life Encyclopedia*, XII [Mammals III] (New York, 1975), p. 69.

42 See Kerry Kilshaw, Christopher Newman, Christina Buesching, James Bunyan and David Macdonald, 'Coordinated Latrine Use by European Badgers, *Meles meles*: Potential Consequences for Territorial Defense', *Journal of Mammalogy*, XC/5 (2009), pp. 1188–98.

43 Richard B. Bernstein, *Thomas Jefferson: The Revolution of Ideas* (New York, 2004), p. 77.

44 Thomas Jefferson, *Notes on the State of Virginia* (Philadelphia, PA, 1801), p. 95.

45 Ibid., p. 99.

46 Meriwether Lewis and William Clark, *The Journals of the Lewis and Clark Expedition: August 30, 1803–August 24, 1804*, ed. Gary E. Moulton (Lincoln, NE, 1986), p. 430. Later in the description Clark

explicitly states that the new badger 'is of the Bear Species'.

47 Paul Russell Cutright, *Lewis and Clark: Pioneering Naturalists*, 2nd edn (Lincoln, NE, 2003), p. 70.

48 By the late 1500s 'New Spain' commentators had already made passing mention of North American badgers in their own colonial invasion accounts. See Bernal Díaz del Castillo, *The Discovery and Conquest of Mexico, 1517–1521* [1567–75] (Mexico City, 1953), pp. 196–7.

49 Ernest Thompson Seton, *Life-Histories of Northern Animals: An Account of the Mammals of Manitoba*, II (New York, 1909), p. 1005.

50 Committee on the Status of Endangered Wildlife in Canada, 'COSEWIC Assessment and Status Report on the American Badger *Taxidea taxus* in Canada' (Ottawa, 2012), pp. i–iv. The primary subspecies are *T. t. taxus, T. t. jacksoni, T. t. jeffersonii* and *T. t. berlandieri*, with *T. t. taxus* the most stable population.

51 Ludwig Heck, quoted in 'The Mustelids', *Grzimek's Animal Life Encyclopedia*, XII [Mammals III], p. 71.

52 Long and Killingley, *Badgers of the World*, pp. 58–9.

53 Mary Louise Perry, 'Notes on a Captive Badger', *Murrelet: A Journal of Northwestern Ornithology and Mammalogy*, XX/3 (September–December 1939), p. 51.

54 Ontario American Badger Recovery Team, 'Draft Recovery Status', p. 8.

55 See Gail R. Michener, 'Hunting Techniques and Tool Use by North American Badgers Preying on Richardson's Ground Squirrels', *Journal of Mammalogy*, LXXXV/5 (October 2004), pp. 1019–27.

56 See Ernest Thompson Seton, *Wild Animals at Home* (Garden City, NY, 1913), pp. 116–30, and Frank Thone, 'Nature Ramblings: Badger', *Science News-Letter*, XV, no. 429 (29 June 1929), p. 411.

57 After Roosevelt's second term in office finished and he returned to politics following a three-year hiatus, the mascot of his upstart Progressive Party was a bull moose, not a badger. He lost the election to the Democratic Woodrow Wilson. Beccy Tanner, 'Pet Kansas Badger Once Roamed White House', *Wichita Eagle*,

10 September 2012, available at www.kansas.com (accessed 12 November 2013).

58 Harold F. Duebbert, 'Swimming by a Badger', *Journal of Mammalogy*, XLVIII/2 (May 1967), p. 323.

59 Bewick, *General History*, 4th edn, p. 284.

60 Daniel Hahn, *The Tower Menagerie: Being the Amazing True Story of the Royal Collection of Wild and Ferocious Beasts* (London, 2003), p. xvii.

61 R. I. Pocock, *The Fauna of British India, Including Ceylon and Burma, Mammalia*, vol. II: *Carnivora* (London, 1941), p. 427.

62 Sy Montgomery, *Search for the Golden Moon Bear: Science and Adventure in Pursuit of a New Species* (White River Junction, VT, 2009), p. 51.

63 Neal and Cheeseman, *Badgers*, p. 234.

64 Long and Killingley, *Badgers of the World*, p. 332.

65 Helgen, Lim and Helgen, 'The Hog-badger is Not an Edentate', pp. 371, 375.

66 Montgomery, *Search for the Golden Moon Bear*, p. 76.

67 Ronald M. Nowak, *Walker's Carnivores of the World* (Baltimore, MD, 2005), p. 166.

68 Helgen, Lim and Helgen, 'The Hog-badger is Not an Edentate', p. 353.

69 'British Blamed for Basra Badgers', BBC News, 12 July 2007, available at http://news.bbc.co.uk (accessed 12 November 2013).

70 Neal and Cheeseman, *Badgers*, p. 245.

71 Catherine Philip, 'Bombs, Guns, Gangs – Now Basra Falls Prey to the Monster Badger', *The Times*, 12 July 2007, available at www.timesonline.co.uk.

72 T. C. McCaskie, 'People and Animals: Constru(ct)ing the Asante Experience', *Africa: Journal of the International African Institute*, LXII/2 (1992), p. 226.

73 For a brief discussion of the reputation of ratel castrations of prey, ibid., p. 226; in response to that oft-cited claim, see Colleen Begg and Keith Begg, 'The Honey Badger: The Truth Behind the Myth Part II', available at http://archive.is/ysBpt (accessed 10 November 2013).

74 Vanderhaar and Yeen Ten Hwang, '*Mellivora capensis*', p. 6.

75 Begg and Begg, 'The Honey Badger: The Truth Behind the Myth, Part II'.

76 Randall L. Eaton, 'A Possible Case of Mimicry in Larger Mammals', *Evolution*, XXX/4 (December 1976), p. 853.

77 Jonathan Kingdon, *East African Mammals: An Atlas of Evolution in Africa*, IIIA: *Carnivores* (Chicago, 1977), p. 87.

78 Eaton, 'A Possible Case', p. 854.

79 *Snake Killers: The Honey Badger of the Kalahari*, National Geographic Television, producers Carol and David Hughes, cinematographers Carol and David Hughes and Colleen and Keith Begg, 2001.

80 Kingdon, *East African Mammals*, p. 89.

81 Vanderhaar and Yeen Ten Hwang, '*Mellivora capensis*', p. 5.

82 'ratel, *n.2*', *Oxford English Dictionary Online*.

83 Vanderhaar and Yeen Ten Hwang, '*Mellivora capensis*', p. 5.

84 Henderson, *The Book of Barely Imagined Beings*, pp. 176–81.

85 Begg and Begg, 'The Truth Behind the Myth, Part II'.

## 2 RISE OF THE DELVERS: THE SYMBOLIC BADGER

1 Jim Crumley, *Badgers on the Highland Edge* (London, 1994), p. 128.

2 James MacKillop, *A Dictionary of Celtic Mythology* (Oxford, 1998), p. 30.

3 Charles A. Long and Carl Arthur Killingley, *The Badgers of the World* (Springfield, IL, 1983), p. 4.

4 'A Syrian Terracotta Bird Rattle and Figure of a Badger', Christie's London, 26–7 October 2004, Sale 7017, Lot 392 online, www.christies.com.

5 S. K. Tiwari, *Riddles of Indian Rockshelter Paintings* (New Delhi, 2000), p. 104–5.

6 Polly Schaafsma, *Indian Rock Art of the Southwest* (Santa Fe, 1980), p. 217.

7 Alex Patterson, *Field Guide to Rock Art Symbols of the Greater Southwest* (Boulder, CO, 1992), p. 46.

8  Burr Cartwright Brundage, *The Fifth Sun: Aztec Gods, Aztec World* (Austin, TX, 1979), p. 120.

9  'Makoyohsokoyi (Story of the Wolf Trail, a.k.a. Milky Way)', Blackfoot Digital Library, Red Crow Community College and the University of Lethbridge, available at http://blackfootdigital-library.com.

10  Eldon Yellowhorn, email communication, April 2010.

11  Peter J. Powell, *Sweet Medicine: The Continuing Role of the Sacred Arrows, the Sun Dance, and the Sacred Buffalo Hat in Northern Cheyenne History*, I (Norman, OK, 1969), p. 439.

12  Vine Deloria, Jr, *The World We Used to Live In: Remembering the Powers of the Medicine Men* (Golden, CO, 2006), p. 2.

13  Alfred L. Kroeber, *The Arapaho* (Lincoln, NE, 1983), p. 419.

14  John Holiday and Robert S. McPherson, *A Navajo Legacy: The Life and Teachings of John Holiday* (Norman, OK, 2005), p. 257.

15  Michael Lomatuway'ma, Lorena Lomatuway'ma and Sidney Namingha, *Hopi Animal Stories*, ed. Ekkehart Malotki (Lincoln, NE, 2001), p. 218.

16  Michael Lomatuway'ma and Ekkehart Malotki, 'Coyote and Badger/*Iisawniqw Honani*', *Hopi Coyote Tales: Istutuwutsi* (Lincoln, NE, 1984), pp. 23–41.

17  'Kwasisonwuuti/The Man-Crazed Woman', *The Bedbugs' Night Dance and Other Hopi Tales of Sexual Encounter*, ed. and trans. Ekkehart Malotki (Lincoln, NE, 1997), pp. 34–47. In this text, Kokopelli is given the more linguistically accurate spelling of Kookopölö.

18  *Medicina de quadripedibus*, ed. Joseph Delcourt (Heidelberg, 1914), pp. 5 and 7.

19  Louis Crompton, *Homosexuality and Civilization* (Cambridge, MA, 2006), p. 279.

20  Joannes Jonstonus [John Johnston], *A Description of the Nature of Four-Footed Beasts, With their Figures Engraved in Brass* (London, 1678), p. 79; available at http://digital.library.wisc.edu (accessed 12 November 2013).

21  Jonathon Green, *Cassell's Dictionary of Slang*, 2nd edn

(London, 2005), p. 52.

22  For examples of current slang terms associating badgers with human genitals and sexual activity see www.urbandictionary.com (accessed 12 November 2013).

23  Robert L. Hall, *An Archaeology of the Soul: North American Indian Belief and Ritual* (Chicago, 1997), p. 183, n. 25.

24  Gerald Milnes, *Signs, Cures, and Witchery: German Appalachian Folklore* (Knoxville, TN, 2007), p. 98.

25  See particularly Graham Harvey, *Animism: Respecting the Living World* (New York, 2006), and Sarah M. Pike, *Earthly Bodies, Magical Selves: Contemporary Pagans and the Search for Community* (Berkeley, CA, 2001).

26  Ted Andrews, *Animal-Speak: The Spiritual and Magical Powers of Creatures Great and Small* (Woodbury, MN, 1996), p. 247.

27  Michael Dylan Foster, *Pandemonium and Parade: Japanese Monsters and the Culture of Yokai* (Berkeley, CA, 2009), pp. 36, 225.

28  Hodukai School, *Badger*, Edo period, Metropolitan Museum of Art online, http://metmuseum.org (accessed 12 November 2013); Hokusai Katsushika, *Bunbuku chagama*, *c*. 1830–50, Library of Congress Prints and Photographs Online Catalog, www.loc.gov (accessed 12 November 2013).

29  Michael Tangemann, email correspondence, 6 August 2010.

30  J. Mark Ramseyer and Minoru Nakazato, *Japanese Law: An Economic Approach* (Chicago, IL, 1999), p. 155.

31  Danika Medak-Saltzman, email correspondence, 7 January 2013.

32  William Sayers, 'Names for the Badger in Multilingual Medieval Britain', *ANQ*, XXII/4 (Fall 2009), p. 5.

33  Keith and Colleen Begg, 'Research: Ongoing Projects', *Honey Badgers* website, 8 April 2004 www.honeybadger.com.

34  '19 Caliber: 19 Badger', James Calhoon Manufacturing, www.jamescalhoon.com (accessed 13 November 2013).

35  Richard L. Miller, *Under the Cloud: The Decades of Nuclear Testing* (The Woodlands, TX, 1991), pp. 166–8.

36  Walter J. Boyne, *Air Warfare: An International Encyclopedia*, I (Santa Barbara, CA, 2002), p. 636.

37  *BAM*, 115th Fighter Wing, Wisconsin Air National Guard, XXXV/8 (October 2009), p. 13.

38  Don Kopriva and Jim Mott, *On Wisconsin!: The History of Badger Athletics* (Champaign, IL, 2001), p. 107. Unfortunately, the authors get the raccoon mascot's name wrong: the actual reverse of 'badger' is Regdab, not Regbad. A UW online archive post provides the correct information: http://uwmadarchives.tumblr.com (accessed 13 November 2013).

39  'Bucky Badger Bio', www.uwbadgers.com (accessed 13 November 2013).

40  Being Bucky official website, www.beingbucky.com (accessed 13 November 2013).

41  R. Lee Sullivan, 'Badger Game', *Forbes*, CLIV/7 (26 September 1994), p. 20.

42  Lt Col Jacqueline Guthrie, Public Affairs Director, Wisconsin National Guard, personal communication, 30 July 2010.

43  A. C. Fox-Davies, *A Complete Guide to Heraldry* (New York, 2007), pp. 17–18.

44  Randle Holme, *The Academy of Armory, or, A Storehouse of Armory and Blazon* (Chester, 1688), p. 131.

45  Sylvanus Morgan, *Armilogia, sive, Ars chromocritica* (London, 1666), p. 202.

46  'The Armorial Bearings of the Bonnington Group,' Bonnington Jumeirah Lakes Towers Dubai official blog, 18 March 2009, http://bonningtontower.wordpress.com (accessed 13 November 2013).

47  'Frontier Airlines Announces Winning Name for Badger', press release, 5 July 2010, www.businesswire.com; 'Animal Tales', Frontier Airlines website, www.flyfrontier.com (accessed 13 November 2013).

48  'Badger's History and Legend', W. S. Badger website, www.badgerbalm.com (accessed 13 November 2013).

49  Ralph Paglia, 'Johnson Automotive Badger Commercials', *Automotive Digital Marketing*, 29 April 2008, www.automotive-digitalmarketing.com (accessed 13 November 2013).

50 Chris Baysden, 'Dealer's Badger Campaign a Departure among Local Spots', *Triangle Business Journal*, 2 November 2007, http://triangle.bizjournals.com (accessed 13 November 2013).

51 Home page, Johnson Automotive website, www.johnsonautomotivecenter.com (accessed 13 November 2013).

52 Home page, Johnson Automotive, Badger Gear, formerly at http://johnsonbadgergear.com.

53 'Randall's Wild Wild World of Animals', http://randallshoneybadger.com (accessed 13 November 2013).

54 Randall, '"Randall's Animals" Does the Pigs of Wall Street', Huffpost Comedy, *Huffington Post*, 15 March 2011, www.huffingtonpost.com (accessed 13 November 2013); Michael Humphrey, 'A Chat with Randall: On Nasty Honey Badgers, Bernie Madoff and Fame', 21 April 2011, http://blogs.forbes.com (accessed 13 November 2013).

55 Lacey Rose, 'Honey Badger Viral Sensation Heading to TV', *Hollywood Reporter*, 17 January 2012, www.hollywoodreporter.com.

3 NOTABLE BADGERS OF PAGE AND SCREEN

1 Kenneth Grahame, *The Wind in the Willows* (London, 1908), pp. 72–3.

2 Ibid., p. 73. There is an interesting parallel between this fictional scene and events in recent history: in 2004 a UK Ministry of Defence archaeologist advocated a badger cull, but not to save cattle or the livelihoods of farmers; rather, it was to protect Iron Age, Bronze Age and Romano-British archaeological sites on Salisbury Plain from being harmed by badger diggings (Malcolm Tait, 'Badger Busting', *The Ecologist*, XXXIV/1 (February 2004), p. 9).

3 Geraldine D. Poss, 'An Epic in Arcadia: The Pastoral World of *The Wind in the Willows*', *Children's Literature*, IV (1975), p. 83.

4 Tess Cosslett, *Talking Animals in British Children's Fiction, 1786–1914* (Aldershot, 2006), pp. 174–5.

5 Robert Hemmings, 'A Taste of Nostalgia: Children's Books from the Golden Age – Carroll, Grahame, and Milne', *Children's Literature*, xxxv (2007), p. 67.

6 Grahame, *Wind in the Willows*, p. 101.

7 See U. C. Knoepflmacher, 'Oscar Wilde at Toad Hall: Kenneth Grahame's Drainings and Draggings', *The Lion and the Unicorn*, xxxiv/1 (January 2010), pp. 1–16.

8 Seth Lerer, 'Style and the Mole: Domestic Aesthetics in *The Wind in the Willows*', *Journal of Aesthetic Education*, xliii/2 (Summer 2009), p. 53.

9 Jan Needle, *Wild Wood* (London, 1981), p. 47.

10 Ibid., p. 77.

11 Marie Nelson, 'Old English Riddle No. 15: The "Badger": An Early Example of Mock Heroic', *Neophilologus*, lix (1975), p. 448.

12 Anne Rooney, *Hunting in Middle English Literature* (Woodbridge, 1993), pp. 16–18.

13 Garry Mavin, 'Unspeakability, Inedibility, and the Structures of Pursuit in the English Foxhunt', *Representing Animals*, ed. Nigel Rothfels (Bloomington, in, 2002), p. 147.

14 John Webster, *The Dramatic Works of John Webster*, ed. William Hazlitt, ii (London, 1857), p. 250.

15 Keith Thomas, *Man and the Natural World: Changing Attitudes in England, 1500–1800* (New York, 1996), p. 15.

16 Quoted in David Perkins, 'Sweet Helpston! John Clare on Badger Baiting', *Studies in Romanticism*, xxxviii/3 (1999), p. 407.

17 Ibid.

18 Ibid., pp. 395–6.

19 Lewis Carroll, *The Annotated Alice*, ed. Martin Gardner (New York, 1960), pp. 269–71.

20 Lewis Carroll, *Sylvie and Bruno* (London and New York, 1889), pp. 248, 253.

21 J.R.R. Tolkien, *The Lord of the Rings*, centenary edition (Boston, ma, 1991), p. 148.

22 In his notes for *The Annotated Hobbit*, Douglas A. Anderson presents some evidence for a linguistic and narrative connection

between the word 'hobbit' and 'rabbit', though Tolkien himself seems to have largely disavowed this connection: 'I must admit that its faint suggestion of *rabbit* appealed to me. Not that hobbits at all resemble rabbits, unless it be in burrowing'. (J.R.R. Tolkien, *The Annotated Hobbit*, ed. Douglas A. Anderson (London, 2003), p. 146, n. 8.) In habit, diet, home and social life, hobbits seem more to resemble badgers than they do rabbits.

23 Tolkien greatly admired *The Wind in the Willows* and offered praise for the 'excellent book' in the notes of his classic essay 'On Fairy-Stories' (J.R.R. Tolkien, *Tree and Leaf, Smith of Wootton Major, The Homecoming of Beorhtnoth*, London, 1975, p. 73).

24 Joseph Bosworth, 'smygel', *An Anglo-Saxon Dictionary*, ed. T. Northcote Toller (Oxford, 1898), p. 890; available at http://bosworth.ff.cuni.cz (accessed 3 July 2010).

25 T. H. White, *The Once and Future King* (New York, 1958), p. 196.

26 T. H. White, *The Book of Merlyn* (Austin, TX, 1977), pp. 33–5.

27 C. S. Lewis, *Prince Caspian* (London, 1951; rep. New York, 2005), p. 73.

28 Leslie Marmon Silko, *Storyteller* (New York, 1981), p. 55.

29 John Hogan, *St Ciaran, Patron of Ossory: A Memoir of his Life and Times* (Kilkenny, 1876), pp. 124–5. See also Helen Waddell, *Beasts and Saints* (London, 1934), pp. 101–6.

30 Kenneth Varty, *Reynard, Renart, Reinaert and Other Foxes in Medieval England: The Iconographic Evidence* (Amsterdam, 1999), pp. 23–30.

31 W. B. Yeats, *The Collected Poems of W. B. Yeats*, ed. Richard J. Finneran, 2nd edn (New York, 2010), p. 321.

32 J. P. Malcolm, *An Historical Sketch of the Art of Caricaturing with Graphic Illustrations* (London, 1813), p. 114; available at http://hdl.handle.net (accessed 14 November 2013).

33 J. K. Rowling, *Harry Potter and the Philosopher's Stone* (London, 2000), p. 88.

34 In an annotation of the first book she wrote, 'Perhaps Hufflepuff house would have the respect it deserves from fans if I'd stayed with my original idea of a bear to represent it?' 'J. K. Rowling,

*Harry Potter and the Philosopher's Stone* – with Annotations',
*The Guardian*, 18 May 2013, www.theguardian.com (accessed
14 November 2013).

35 Farah Mendelsohn, 'Crowning the King: Harry Potter and the
Construction of Authority', in *The Ivory Tower and Harry Potter:
Perspectives on a Literary Phenomenon*, ed. Lana A. Whited
(Columbia, MI, 2002), p. 171.

36 'J. K. Rowling Web Chat Transcript', *The Leaky Cauldron*, 30 July
2007, www.the-leaky-cauldron.org (accessed 14 November 2013).
Online fans have noted the similarity between the decor of the
Hufflepuff common room and the comfortable underworld
abodes of Mr Badger from *The Wind in the Willows* and Bilbo
Baggins from Tolkien's works: Chamber of Secrets discussion
thread, 'Hufflepuff Common Room', www.cosforums.com.

37 The BB Society, www.welford.org/bb (accessed 14 November 2013).

38 Brian Jacques, *The Tribes of Redwall: Badgers* (New York, 2001), p. 1.

39 Bruce Weber, 'Russell Hoban, "Frances" Author, Dies at 86', *New
York Times*, 14 December 2011, www.nytimes.com (accessed 14
November 2013).

40 N. Scott Momaday, *House Made of Dawn* (New York, 1969), pp. 34
and 62.

41 The Great Sioux Nation is composed of three primary linguistic
groupings: Lakota, Nakota and Dakota. Zitkala-Ša's people, the
Yankton Sioux, are Dakota speakers.

42 Zitkala-Ša, *Iktomi and the Ducks and Other Sioux Stories*, ed. P. Jane
Hafen (Lincoln, NE, 1985, repr. 2004), pp. 62–4.

43 Ibid., pp. 71–2.

44 Ibid., p. 73.

45 Ernest Thompson Seton, *Wild Animals at Home* (New York, 1913),
pp. 128–9.

46 Jace Weaver, *That the People Might Live: Native American Literatures
and Native American Community* (New York, 1997), p. 207 n. 66.

47 Lopez, *Crow and Weasel*, p. 59.

48 Annie Proulx, 'The Old Badger Game', *Bad Dirt: Wyoming Stories 2*
(New York, 2004), p. 89.

49  Christina Rossetti, 'Goblin Market' [1862] (London, 1893), pp. 1, 5, 11.
50  Alan Ritchie, *Ruark Remembered: By the Man Who Knew Him Best* (Columbia, SC, 2006), pp. 133–4.
51  Angela Cassidy, 'Vermin, Victims and Disease: UK Framings of Badgers in and beyond the Bovine TB Controversy', *Sociologia Ruralis*, LII/2 (April 2012), p. 205.
52  'What Badgers Eat', www.thesimpsons.com, (accessed 10 November 2013)
53  James Lowder and Voronica Whitney-Robinson, *Spectre of the Black Rose* (Renton, WA, 1999), p. 15.
54  See also James Lowder, *Knight of the Black Rose* (Lake Geneva, WI, 1991) and Andrew Cermak, John W. Mangrum and Andrew Wyatt, *Ravenloft Core Rulebook* (Atlanta, GA, 2001), pp. 139–40.


4  USES AND ABUSES: THE PERSECUTED BADGER

 1  Timothy J. Roper, *Badger* (London, 2010), pp. 32–3.
 2  John Barrow, *An Account of Travels into the Interior of Southern Africa, in the Years 1797 and 1798*, I (London, 1801), p. 335.
 3  Walter W. Dalquest, 'Additional Notes on Mammals from Mozambique', *Journal of Mammalogy*, XLIX/1 (February 1968), p. 117.
 4  Veerle Linseele and Wim Van Neer, 'Exploitation of Desert and Other Wild Game in Ancient Egypt: The Archaeological Evidence from the Nile Valley', in *Desert Animals in the Eastern Sahara*, ed. Heiko Reimer, Frank Förster, Michael Herb and Nadja Pöllath (Cologne, 2009), p. 66.
 5  Johann Schröder, *Zoologia; or, The history of animals as they are useful in physick and chirurgery* (London, 1659), p. 79; W. Mather, *A very useful manual, or, The young mans companion* (London, 1681), p. 109.
 6  Charles Estienne, *Maison rustique, or The countrey farme* (London, 1616), p. 457.
 7  Joannes Jonstonus (John Johnston), *A Description of the Nature of Four-Footed Beasts, With their Figures Engraved in Brass* (London, 1678), p. 79; available at http://digital.library.wisc.edu (accessed 12 November 2013).

8 Hans Kruuk, *Hunter and Hunted: Relationships between Carnivores and People* (Cambridge, 2002), pp. 118–19.

9 Ibid., p. 119.

10 Tom Jaine, quoted in Alan Davidson, *The Oxford Companion to Food*, 2nd edn (Oxford, 2006), p. 51.

11 Martin Schmitt, '"Meat's Meat": An Account of the Flesh-Eating Habits of Western Americans', *Western Folklore*, XI/3 (July 1952), p. 187.

12 Colleen Begg and Keith Begg, 'The Honey Badger: The Truth Behind the Myth, Part II', available at http://archive.is/ysBpt (accessed 10 November 2013)

13 'Wonderland: The Man Who Eats Badgers and Other Strange Tales', directed by Daniel Vernon, BBC Two, 2008.

14 N. N. Ozeretskovaskaya, L. G. Mikhailova, T. P. Sabgaida and A. S. Dovgalev, 'New Trends and Clinical Patterns of Human Trichinellosis in Russia at the Beginning of the XXI Century', *Veterinary Parasitology*, 132 (2005), p. 170.

15 Roper, *Badger*, p. 33.

16 Ernest Thompson Seton, *Life-Histories of Northern Animals: An Account of the Mammals of Manitoba* (New York, 1909), I, p. 1009.

17 Matt Peek, Kansas Department of Wildlife and Parks Furharvester Activity Summary, 2011–12, State of Kansas, p. 2; Sam Wilson, Nebraska Game and Parks Commission, Fur Harvest Survey, 2011/2012 season, 3 August 2012.

18 North American Fur Auctions, March 2010 Wild Fur Sale report, pp. 2–4, www.nafa.ca (accessed 14 November 2013).

19 Desmond Morris, *Intimate Behavior: A Zoologist's Classic Study of Human Intimacy* [1971] (New York, 1997), p. 38.

20 Charles A. Long and Carl Arthur Killingley, *The Badgers of the World* (Springfield, IL, 1983), p. 13.

21 'Bristle Styles and Additional Information', Em's Place, Inc., www.emsplace.com (accessed 14 November 2013).

22 Xavier Domingo-Roura, Josep Marmi, Aïnhoa Ferrando, Francesc López-Giráldez, David W. Macdonald and Hugh A. H. Jansman, 'Badger Hair in Shaving Brushes Comes from Protected Eurasian Badgers', *Biological Conservation*, CXXVIII/3 (March 2006), pp. 425–30.

23  Mary E. Fissell, 'Imagining Vermin in Early Modern England', in *The Animal/Human Boundary: Historical Perspectives*, ed. Angela N. H. Creager and William Chester Jordan (Rochester, NY, 2002), p. 77.

24  Angela Cassidy, 'Vermin, Victims and Disease: UK Framings of Badgers in and Beyond the Bovine TB Controversy', *Sociologia Ruralis*, LII/2 (April 2012), p. 203.

25  *The Vermin-Killer: Being a Compleat and Necessary Family-Book . . .* (London, 1765?), p. 27.

26  Ibid., p. 8.

27  Solomon Bogale, 'Indigenous Knowledge and its Relevance for sustainable Beekeeping Development: A Case Study in the Highlands of Southeast Ethiopia', *Livestock Research for Rural Development*, 21 (11) 2009, article 184, http://www.lrrd.org (accessed 13 June 2010).

28  Tobie Wharton, 'Honey Badger: Friend or Foe?', *Biological Sciences Review*, XVIII/4 (April 2006), pp. 18–27.

29  Keith Begg and Colleen Begg, 'The Conflict Between Beekeepers and Honey Badgers in South Africa: A Western Cape Perspective', *Open Country*, 4 (Summer 2002), pp. 26–7.

30  International Union for Conservation of Nature, *Mellivora capensis*, The IUCN Red List of Threatened Species (2013.1), www.iucnredlist.org (accessed 14 November 2013).

31  Committee on the Status of Endangered Wildlife in Canada, 'COSEWIC Assessment and Status Report on the American Badger *Taxidea taxus* in Canada' (Ottawa, 2012), pp. 32–3.

32  Ontario American Badger Recovery Team, Draft Recovery Strategy for the American Badger (*Taxidea taxus*) in Ontario (Peterborough, ON: Ontario Ministry of Natural Resources, 2009), pp. 9–10.

33  Trevor A. Kinley and Nancy J. Newhouse, 'Badger Roadkill Risk in Relation to the Presence of Culverts and Jersey Barriers', *Northwest Science*, LXXXIII/2 (2009), p. 148.

34  Timur Moon, 'Far-Right Extremists Chased Through London by Women Dressed as Badgers', *International Business Times*, 1 June 2013, www.ibtimes.co.uk (accessed 14 November 2013).

35  The Center for Food Security and Public Health, 'Bovine

Tuberculosis Fact Sheet', Iowa State University College of Veterinary Medicine, Ames, IA, 2007, p. 2.

36 Rosie Woodroffe et al., 'Bovine Tuberculosis in Cattle and Badgers in Localized Culling Areas', *Journal of Wildlife Diseases*, XLV/1 (2009), p. 128; Nigel Williams, 'Threatened Badgers Breeding Secrets', *Current Biology*, XVI/7 (4 April 2006), p. R232, available at www.sciencedirect.com (accessed 14 November 2013).

37 'In for the Cull', *Nature*, CDL/7166 (1 November 2007), available at www.nature.com (accessed 14 November 2013).

38 Cassidy, 'Vermin, Victims and Disease', pp. 194, 195.

39 Ibid., p. 198.

40 Hugh Warwick, *The Beauty in the Beast: Britain's Favourite Creatures and the People Who Love Them* (London, 2012), pp. 28–9.,

41 Mark Jones et al., 'Animal Welfare Concerns Related to Badger Culling', open letter to Rt Hon. Owen Paterson, MP, Secretary of State for Environment, Food and Rural Affairs, 12 October 2012, www.hsi.org (accessed 14 November 2013).

42 Damian Carrington, 'Humaneness of Badger Cull to be Judged by Noise of Dying Animals', *Guardian* online, 30 May 2013, www.theguardian.com, viewed 15 May 2014.

43 Independent Scientific Group on Cattle TB (ISG), 'Bovine TB: The Scientific Evidence, A Science Base for a Sustainable Policy to Control TB in Cattle, An Epidemiological Investigation into Bovine Tuberculosis', Final Report of the Independent Scientific Group on Cattle TB', Department for Environment, Food and Rural Affairs, June 2007, p. 5.

44 Alistair Driver, 'The Badger Culling Debate', *Farmers Guardian*, 2 November 2007, www.farmersguardian.com (accessed 14 November 2013).

45 Roper, *Badger*, pp. 324–5; 'First Tuberculosis Vaccine for Badgers is Authorized', press release, Veterinary Laboratories Agency and the Food and Environment Research Agency, 30 March 2010.

46 See W. Ray Waters, M. V. Palmer, B. M. Buddle and H. Martin Vordermeier, 'Bovine Tuberculosis Vaccine Research: Historical Perspectives and Recent Advances', *Vaccine*, XXX (2012), pp. 2611–22.

47 Jacqueline Simpson and Steve Roud, 'blood sports', *A Dictionary of English Folklore* (Oxford, 2000).

48 Linda Kalof, *Looking at Animals in Human History* (London, 2007), p. 89.

49 James Turner, *Reckoning with the Beast: Animals, Pain, and Humanity in the Victorian Mind* (Baltimore, 1980), p. 20.

50 Thomas Bewick, *A General History of Quadrupeds*, 4th edn (Newcastle upon Tyne, 1800), pp. 281–2.

51 Long and Killingley, *Badgers of the World*, p. 20.

52 Garry Marvin, 'Unspeakability, Inedibility, and the Structures of Pursuit in the English Foxhunt', in *Representing Animals* (Bloomington, IN, 2002), p. 140. For a sympathetic but informative description of badger digging, see H. H. King, *Working Terriers, Badgers and Badger Digging* (London, 1931, repr. Cook Hill, Warwickshire, 2005).

53 Andy Shipp, testimony, 7 March 2012, House of Commons Environmental Audit Committee, Wildlife Crime, Third Report of Session 2012–2013, vol. I (London, 2012), p. Ev. 7.

54 David Perkins, 'Sweet Helpston! John Clare on Badger Baiting', *Studies in Romanticism*, XXXVIII/3 (1999), p. 388.

55 Simpson and Roud, 'blood sports'.

56 Kathleen Kete, 'Animals and Ideology: The Politics of Animal Protection in Europe', in *Representing Animals*, ed. Nigel Rothfels (Madison, WI, 2002), pp. 26–7.

57 Robert Smith, 'Investigating Financial Aspects of Dog-fighting in the UK', *Journal of Financial Crime*, XCIII/4 (2011), p. 339.

58 Shipp, testimony, 7 March 2012, Environmental Audit Committee, p. Ev. 2, 6.

59 'Cruelty to Badgers "Almost Doubles" Ahead of Cull', BBC News UK, 14 April 2013, www.bbc.co.uk (accessed 14 November 2013).

60 Seton, *Life-Histories of Northern Animals*, II, pp. 1000–1001.

1 While Drabble intended this term to be a reference to *Meles meles*, it is an unfortunate neologism, for not only did he not coin *melophilia*, the word actually refers to a love of music, with *melomania* a 'frantic fondness' and *melophobia* an 'aversion' (see Jacob Edward Schmidt, *Reversicon: A Medical Word Finder*, Ann Arbor, MI, 1958, p. 245). Dr John Aveline, a professional Latinist, suggested 'meliphilia (and the anglicized meliphile)' as the more appropriate Latin forms of Drabble's ailment (personal correspondence, 18 March 2014).

2 Known as Gillette Flats, this area was the 1895 location for Colorado's sole bullfight during the height of the Gold Rush; in the nearby Pinnacle Park, bears, mountain lions and other unfortunate beasts were kept in a makeshift zoo as entertainment for the miners. A brief walk from the road could take observers to the shallow concrete pits that remained until the local mine levelled the area a few years ago (Cripple Creek District Museum, *The Cripple Creek District*, Charleston, SC, 2011, pp. 36, 46).

3 My dad recalls having killed two badgers with a rat-tailed file when he was a boy living on his family's ranch in eastern Colorado in the 1930s. He did this in part just to see if he could. Fortunately he has softened considerably toward the animal world in the ensuing years.

4 For a summary of the legal status of badgers in the UK, see Ernest Neal and Chris Cheeseman, *Badgers* (London, 1996), pp. 249–52.

5 Timothy J. Roper, *Badger* (London, 2010), p. 40.

6 'About Us', The Badger Trust, www.badger.org.uk (accessed 14 November 2013).

7 Cape Nature Conservation, 'Badgers and Beekeepers', www.capenature.co.za (accessed 14 November 2013); 'Badger and Beekeeper', The Honey Badger, www.honeybadger.com (accessed 13 November 2013).

8 Ronald M. Nowak, *Walker's Carnivores of the World* (Baltimore, MD, 2005), pp. 167–9.

9 Committee on the Status of Endangered Wildlife in Canada, 'COSEWIC Assessment and Status Report on the American Badger

*Taxidea taxus* in Canada' (Ottawa, 2012), pp. 22–5.

10  Ontario American Badger Recovery Team, 'Recovery Strategy for the American Badger (*Taxidea taxus*) in Ontario', Ontario Recovery Strategy Series, Ontario Ministry of Natural Resources (Peterborough, ON, 2010), pp. iv, 3. These figures were further confirmed in the 2012 'COSEWIC Assessment and Status Report', p. iii.

11  Patrick Barkham, *Badgerlands: The Twilight World of Britain's Most Enigmatic Mammal* (London, 2013), p. 356.

12  Ernest Neal, *The Natural History of Badgers* (London, 1986), p. 223.

13  Ibid.

# Select Bibliography

Barkham, Patrick, *Badgerlands: The Twilight World of Britain's Most Enigmatic Animal* (London, 2013)

Buffon, Comte de (Georges-Louis Leclerc), *Natural History: General and Particular*, trans. William Smellie (London, 1781)

Cassidy, Angela, 'Vermin, Victims and Disease: UK Framings of Badgers in and Beyond the Bovine TB Controversy', *Sociologia Ruralis*, LII/2 (April 2012), pp. 192–214

Clark, Michael, *Badgers* (Stowmarket, 1988, revd edn 2010)

Committee on the Status of Endangered Wildlife in Canada, 'COSEWIC Assessment and Status Report on the American Badger *Taxidea taxus* in Canada' (Ottawa, 2012), pp. i–63

Crumley, Jim, *Badgers on the Highland Edge* (London, 1994)

Cuvier, Baron (Georges), *The Animal Kingdom, Arranged According to its Organization, Serving as a Foundation for the Natural History of Animals, and an Introduction to Comparative Anatomy* (London, 1834)

Dragoo, Jerry W., and Rodney L. Honeycutt, 'Systematics of Mustelid-like Carnivores', *Journal of Mammalogy*, LXXVIII/2 (May 1997), pp. 426–43

Drabble, Phil, *Badgers at my Window* (London, 1969, repr. Brookland, Kent, 1989)

—, *No Badgers in My Wood* (London, 1979)

Grahame, Kenneth, *The Wind in the Willows* (London, 1908)

Griffiths, Huw I., ed., *Mustelids in a Modern World: Management and Conservation Aspects of Small Carnivore: Human Interactions* (Leiden, 2000)

Helgen, Kristofer M., Norman T.-L. Lim and Lauren E. Helgen, 'The Hog-badger Is Not an Edentate: Systematics and Evolution of the Genus *Arctonyx* (Mammalia: Mustelidae)', *Zoological Journal of the Linnaean Society*, CLVIII (2008), pp. 353–85

Independent Scientific Group on Cattle TB (ISG), 'Bovine TB: The Scientific Evidence, A Science Base for a Sustainable Policy to Control TB in Cattle, An Epidemiological Investigation into Bovine Tuberculosis', Final Report of the Independent Scientific Group on Cattle TB, Department for Environment, Food and Rural Affairs (June 2007)

*Jeffersonii* Badger Recovery Team, 'Recovery Strategy for the Badger (*Taxidea taxus*) in British Columbia', British Columbia Ministry of the Environment (Victoria, BC, September 2008)

Kalof, Linda, *Looking at Animals in Human History* (London, 2007)

Kete, Kathleen, 'Animals and Ideology: The Politics of Animal Protection in Europe', *Representing Animals*, ed. Nigel Rothfels (Madison, WI, 2002), pp. 19–34.

Kingdon, Jonathan, *East African Mammals: An Atlas of Evolution in Africa*, IIIA: Carnivores (Chicago, 1977)

Kinley, Trevor A., and Nancy J. Newhouse, 'Badger Roadkill Risk in Relation to the Presence of Culverts and Jersey Barriers', *Northwest Science*, LXXXIII/2 (2009), p. 148

Koepfli, Klaus-Peter, et al., 'Multigene Phylogeny of the Mustelidae: Resolving Relationships, Tempo and Biogeographic History of a Mammalian Adaptive Radiation', *BMC Biology*, VI/1 (2008), pp. 10–22

Kruuk, Hans, *Hunter and Hunted: Relationships between Carnivores and People* (Cambridge, 2002)

Long, Charles A., '*Taxidea taxus*', *Mammalian Species*, 26 (13 June 1973), pp. 1–4

—, and Carl Arthur Killingley, *The Badgers of the World* (Springfield, IL, 1983)

Mills, Gus, and Lex Hes, *The Complete Book of Southern African Mammals* (Cape Town, 1997)

Neal, Ernest, *The Natural History of Badgers* (London, 1986)

—, and Chris Cheeseman, *Badgers* (London, 1996)

Nowak, Ronald M., *Walker's Carnivores of the World* (Baltimore, 2005)

Ontario American Badger Recovery Team, 'Draft Recovery Status for the American Badger (*Taxidea taxus*) in Ontario' (Peterborough, ON, 2009)

Owen, Pamela R., 'Description of a New Late Miocene American Badger (Taxidiinae) Utilizing High-resolution X-ray Computed Tomography', *Palaeontology*, XLIX/5 (2006), pp. 999–1011

Perkins, David, 'Sweet Helpston! John Clare on Badger Baiting', *Studies in Romanticism*, XXXVIII/3 (1999), pp. 387–407

Roper, Timothy J., *Badger* (London, 2010)

Seton, Ernest Thompson, *Life-histories of Northern Animals: An Account of the Mammals of Manitoba*, II (New York, 1909)

—, *Wild Animals at Home* (Garden City, NY, 1913)

*Snake Killers: The Honey Badger of the Kalahari*, National Geographic Television, producers Carol and David Hughes, cinematographers Carol and David Hughes and Colleen and Keith Begg, 2001

Turner, James, *Reckoning with the Beast: Animals, Pain, and Humanity in the Victorian Mind* (Baltimore, 1980)

Vanderhaar, Jana M., and Yeen Ten Hwang, '*Mellivora capensis*', *Mammalian Species*, 721 (30 July 2003), pp. 1–8

Zitkala-Ša, *Iktomi and the Ducks and Other Sioux Stories*, ed. P. Jane Hafen (Lincoln, NE, 2004)

# Associations and Websites

The Badger Trust

www.badger.org.uk

The home of the UK's most active and effective badger advocacy group, the Badger Trust site is an excellent resource for those interested in the animals' protection and educating themselves and others about the benefits of living with badgers. In addition to media releases and educational materials about the current conditions for badgers in the UK (and to a lesser degree elsewhere in Europe), the site includes an online gift shop, membership and donation links, and links to local badger groups.

Badgerland

www.badgerland.co.uk

Advertised as 'The definitive factually-accurate on-line guide to badgers in the UK', this site offers various resources for Eurasian badger enthusiasts, including information about badger activism, advice for observing the animals in the wild and for dealing with problem badgers in gardens, a photo gallery, diverse literature and badger-themed gifts.

The Honey Badger

www.honeybadger.com

Easy to navigate, informative and well-designed, featuring the scholarship, photography and video work of famed ratel researchers Keith and Colleen Begg, this is the best site for research about honey badgers. It includes media downloads, information about conservation issues, badger-friendly honey and other relevant materials. A number of the Beggs' scientific papers are available as downloadable PDFS.

The Nature Conservancy of Canada (NCC)
www.natureconservancy.ca
Canada's leading land conservation organization, and an influential force in protecting vulnerable North American badger habitat. Since 1962 the NCC has helped to protect more than 800,000 hectares of ecologically significant land nationwide. All author royalties for this book are being donated to the NCC's badger habitat recovery efforts.

# Acknowledgements

This book simply would not exist if not for the support of a community of family, friends, colleagues and even strangers, who all shared generosity beyond expectation. A particular note of gratitude to Reaktion publisher Michael Leaman and editors Jonathan Burt and Martha Jay for their support through the unexpectedly long process – thanks for not giving up on me! Deep appreciation to Sophie Mayer, Sara Salih, Kyle Wyatt, Mareike Neuhaus and Tereska Jagiełło, Andrew Yang, Jessica Lockhart, Jenna Hunnef, Bryan Talbot, Simon Flory, Hugh Warwick, Linda Grussani, Sam and Karen Morrison, June Scudeler and Tol Foster for directing me to some amazing references and images; Eldon Yellowhorn, David Cornsilk, Joseph Bruchac, Simon Ortiz, Rick Pouliot, Rauna Kuokkanen, Tracy Cheng, Michael Tangemann, and Sophie again for helping me with names and translations; David Badger, Dale Gienow and Laura Gallagher of the Muskoka Wildlife Centre, Laura Bottaro and Jeff Rife of the Oklahoma City Zoo, Nancy J. Newhouse, Danika Medak-Saltzman, and Chris Stinson and the staff at the UBC Beatty Biodiversity Museum, for their generous professional expertise; LeAnne Howe, Jim Wilson, and all the Salon Ada crew, for unceasing writing encouragement; Lt Col. Jacqueline Guthrie and the Wisconsin National Guard, Susan Kirby, Cindy Van Matre, Adam Phillips, Nobu Tamura, Barbara Heller of the Werner Forman Archive, for help with sourcing images; Erin Griffin, for her amazing beadwork, Kat Moyou, for her excellent art and design, and Meghan Aube, for her fabulous felting; and miscellaneous assistance, badger-themed gifts and support from many of the above as well as Laurie Wells, James Cox, Michelle St John, Alice Te Punga Somerville, Terry Bennett and Justin Lee, Bonnie Breadner and Don, Molly, Riley, and Alex Farquhar, Craig Lampman, Tanya Bob, Jie Ie Baik, Keavy Martin and Richard Van Camp, Deanna Kreisel and Scott MacKenzie, Margery Fee, Coll Thrush, Vin Nardizzi, David Chang and Andrea Santer (aka Honey Badger). Special thanks, too, to Erica Baker and Matthew Norris, whose excellent work and personal enthusiasm as research assistants made possible the organizing, sourcing and permissions process for images, as well as John Hicks, Bryan Talbot, Van Arno, Xhico, Alan Syliboy, Stephen Somers, David Thompson, Andrew Birch, Gorgonio Candelaria Castro, Marianne Carlson, Janice Seline, Ann Japenga, Gary Fillmore, Harvey Leake, Cynthia Chavez Lamar, David Morrison and Alan Bostock, Elizabeth Yake, Sam E. Simpson, Jr and Stephen Radney-Macfarland, Sam and Karen Morrison, Keith Hutchin and Jeff Hayden of the Badger Trust, and Derek van der Merwe and Kelly Marnewick of the Endangered Wildlife Trust.

Living with an academic is not always easy, but I have been blessed to have a family that fully supports my dreams and also keeps me firmly grounded. They have always encouraged this project, even when I was preoccupied with badger minutiae for many hours at a time, even on vacation or days off. My parents, Kathy and Jim Justice, are now and have always been my first fans and best critics, and their support has made all the difference. My deepest thanks, as always, go to my husband, Kent Dunn, who has done more than anyone to hold me up, share the joys and struggles of the project, and celebrate the often weird and wonderful world of badgers with me. Words are inadequate to express my gratitude, and my love.

There are likely many more unacknowledged debts, so my apologies to anyone I may have inadvertently left out of the list. Please know that you have helped make this dream a reality. *Wado, nigada.*

# Photo Acknowledgements

The author and the publishers wish to express their thanks to the below sources of illustrative material and/or permission to reproduce it. The author and publisher have made every effort to respect Indigenous cultural protocols regarding public representation of ceremonial objects. Only images of art pieces made for the commercial market, non-ritual objects or those without known prohibitions have been included. Corrections are welcome for future editions.

Alamy: p. 139 top left (MangoImages); Ardea: p. 64 (Masahiro Iijima); image courtesy of Van Arno: p. 118; courtesy of the Division of Anthropology, American Museum of Natural History: p. 83 (Artifact #50.2/6830A); photographs by author: pp. 11, 143; David Badger: p. 181; courtesy of The Badger Trust: p. 189 centre right; Biosphoto: p. 158 (Alain Dragesco-Joffé); image courtesy of Bonnington Group, Ltd: p. 96 bottom right; © 2006 Box TV/Muse Entertainment Enterprises/ MediaPro Pictures: p. 109; image courtesy of Biodiversity Heritage Library, http://www.biodiversitylibrary.org: pp. 62, 73; courtesy of Andrew Birch: p. 163; Bodleian Library, University of Oxford: p. 21; Bridgeman Images: pp. 19 bottom (private collection/Roy Miles Fine Art Paintings), 20 (private collection/photo © Bonhams, London, UK), 31 (Universal History Archive/UIG), 67 (Zoological Society of London), 74 top, 170 (private collection/The Stapleton Collection), 112 (Bibliothèque Mazarine, Paris, France/Archives Charmet), 144 (private collection/photo © Christie's Images), 152 (private collection/ © Gavin Graham Gallery, London, UK), 178 (private collection); © The

# Index